Advent

Advent is a magic time. It holds all the sweet, almost unbearable anticipation of Christmas for days on end and it's such a big part of our life each year that we treat it as a fifth season. It starts on the fourth Sunday before Christmas and sits snugly in between autumn and the winter solstice (give or take a day or two).

Advent celebrations, of which baking is a vital part, are synonymous with German winter culture. The Christmas cookbooks come down off the shelves around about the same time as the thick coats come out of the wardrobes. Each day throughout Advent friends and neighbours visit each other to exchange packets of homemade cookies wrapped up with ribbons. *Kaffee und Kuchen* takes on a new meaning during this time, when every German household offers up a *Bunter Teller* – a colourful plate of Advent biscuits (cookies) alongside the coffee. The conversation around the table is generally led by the festive biscuits, and in the spirit of Advent it isn't uncommon to leave the house with a new recipe or two tucked into your bag.

The Advent season is steeped in tradition and rituals and, just like the astronomical seasons, much of it is centred around light. The Advent wreath, traditionally a doughnut-shaped circle made of twisted pine branches, sits on our kitchen table and is adorned with four candles. Each candle represents the weekly run-up to Christmas and is lit at mealtimes, providing precious light and warmth during the shortening days.

A slightly less obvious but equally symbolic, and arguably more important, sign of festivities is the oven – constantly aglow in our home during this period, scenting the house with cinnamon, ginger, cardamom, clove and anise as tray upon tray of mouth-watering biscuits bake. It is this smell, of biscuits, spice, candles and pine combined, that is so unique to Advent.

Lebkuchen are the first biscuits to fill the kitchen with the presence of Advent. They're one of the more traditional bakes, engulfed in history and sweetened with honey. Cinnamon stars with a cap of snowy white frosting, meltingly soft vanilla and butter crescent moons, jam-filled ginger hearts, caraway and lemon stars with icing that shatters between your teeth like a thin layer of ice, hazelnut and coconut macaroons, rum truffles, *Dominosteine*, marzipan-filled *Stollen*, gingerbread houses dripping with candied fruit and sugar icicles, chocolate-dipped *Spritzgebäck* and many more biscuits and sweet treats soon follow suit.

The glass jars on our kitchen shelves transform from their everyday job of housing basic dry ingredients into a fairy-tale wall of sugar and spice, each jar filled with a different biscuit that instantly transports us to snowy Bavarian towns and twinkling Christmas markets.

Much of the baking of *Adventsgebäck* is done together as a family. It's a messy affair with icing sugar flying through the air, sprinkles and silver balls skittling around the table and, as you can imagine, much excitement. Never is our oven used more than during the run-up to Christmas. As we hunker and snuggle around the stove each day, we are entertained, warmed and comforted by it. If ever there were a time for the oven to prove its worth as the real hearth of our home, Advent is it.

Bunter Teller

A *Bunter Teller* directly translated means colourful plate and it is in fact a colourful plate of Advent biscuits (cookies), probably one of the most 'German' of German traditions and something that no household in the country is without during the month of December.

Making homemade biscuits, even for those of us who never normally bake, becomes a national pastime at the end of November and throughout the last month of the year, so that the supply of *Weihnachtsplätzchen* (Christmas biscuits) intended to see you through the Advent period never runs out. The order in which they are baked acts as a calendar, a countdown measured in biscuits. The butter-less biscuits, many of them old-fashioned varieties such as *Lebkuchen*, which keep the longest, are baked first, followed by nut biscuits, then macaroons and meringues. We bake butter-rich ones such as *Vanillekipferl* after all of the aforementioned, and finally the last things we make are all the sweets and truffles. The biscuits are usually stored in a towering stack of tins kept at the ready to plate a selection up whenever neighbours and friends pop round.

One of the things I enjoy most about visiting friends during this period is the quiet sense of pride that ascends as the *Bunter Teller* is placed on the table. It's inevitable that every biscuit has a story, usually attached to a person, and as each biscuit is carefully selected and eaten the stories and recipes unfold along with them.

Much like decorating a Christmas tree, putting together a *Bunter Teller* is a seasonal necessity that is both bound by ritual and habit, yet open to new additions. Choosing what biscuits end up on the plate is not too dissimilar to how one might choose cheeses for a cheeseboard – a selection that is varied in both taste and texture and 'something for everyone' is the general rule of thumb.

On Christmas Eve in our house I tailor-make an individual *Bunter Teller* for everyone in the family; these include sweets (candies) and confections as well as biscuits and are placed under or near the tree for all-night grazing purposes. It's also commonplace to add a satsuma to each plate and a handful of nuts to be cracked open using a traditional *Nußknacker*. As a child I can honestly say I was more excited about the prospect of what I might find on my *Bunter Teller* than about everything else under the tree, and it's still true today.

The most memorable *Bunter Teller* I've ever received, though, was during the Christmas of 1999 when I lived in Beijing. Far away from family and missing the familiar build-up, rituals and traditions of Christmas at home, my roommate Jenny and I spent hours soothing each other's homesickness by talking about these very things, hopeful that bringing them alive in conversation would make us feel surrounded by them in person.

I spent Christmas Eve teaching small children (all blissfully unaware of the day's significance) English. Despite not being all that late, it was already dark as I left the classroom and made my way alone back to our room, through the biting-cold wind, scarf pulled up over my mouth and nose, thinking of the annual family Christmas walk to the beach that I wasn't on.

Feeling low and close to tears, I turned the key in the lock to room 508 and pushed open the squeaky scuffed door to a room aglow with candles arranged in an almost shrine like manner surrounding a *Bunter Teller*. 'Surprise!' beamed Jenny with her arms held out, and as we hugged I cried and laughed and gulped in the beauty of the moment – it was everything. I felt like I was home.

Unusually for me, I didn't really give a damn about what was on the plate. As it turns out, while I was teaching, Jenny had spent the day traipsing around the freezing city on an elusive European biscuit hunt. An hour before the shops shut she ended up finding a Lebanese bakery in the embassy area of town, where she bought a platter of *baklava*. And in a last-ditch attempt to make a *Bunter Teller* that was more than just that, she begged at a hotel kitchen and came away with some sort of Danish butter biscuits, all of which she arranged lovingly on a plate awaiting my return.

We Germans take our Advent baking seriously and the pinnacle of it all is the *Bunter Teller*. To be obsessed by the task in hand, though, and to take a selection of biscuits too seriously, is to miss the point entirely. A *Bunter Teller* is as much about the sentiment of coming together around a table to rejoice in life, light and friendship as it is about good biscuits. And ever since 1999 I like to add some totally untraditional, yet unequivocally traditional-to-me *baklava* to my *Bunter Teller*, to remind myself of just that.

Nikolaus – St Nicholas Day

On 5th December children across Germany are incredibly busy – diligently polishing their shoes and tidying their bedrooms in preparation for the arrival of *Nikolaus*.

St Nicholas usually comes under the cover of darkness to deliver small gifts and edible treats to children who have been well behaved. Up and down the country children place their shoes or boots next to the door or window, or on the stairs, in the hope that on waking the next morning they will find them filled. In many ways it's like a stocking, except usually it's just one small, inexpensive gift and mainly sweet treats, fruit and nuts.

This tradition is based on the story of a bishop called *Nikolaus*, who was born in Myra (then Greece, now Turkey). *Nikolaus* was said to have spread kindness wherever he went, occasionally performing miracles and distributing gifts among poor children, hence now being known as the Patron Saint of Children.

Nikolaus is usually accompanied by *Knecht Ruprecht*, who is a dark, demonic character sent to offset the balance and scare children. The idea of *Knecht Ruprecht* filled me with dread as a child (he's basically the devil personified), and to avoid nightmares our mother told us that *Knecht Ruprecht* wouldn't be accompanying *Nikolaus* to our house. Instead, though, *Nikolaus* would carry a sack of coal along with his presents and if we hadn't been good we would receive a sooty black lump in place of a gift. I follow the coal tradition too now that I have small children of my own – clinging onto the idea of *Knecht Ruprecht* isn't worth the sleepless nights.

I will admit, too, that I fail to maintain the boot cleaning part of the tradition – usually we leave muddy wellies or scuffed skate shoes on our stairs, much to the horror of my mum. As I explain to the boys each year, though, clean shoes don't make a good person.

Heiligabend – Christmas Eve

Christmas Eve morning in Germany is usually taken up with last-minute preparations and it can feel a little frantic, but come lunchtime the atmosphere is relaxed and *gemütlich* (cosy), for this is when the festivities begin.

The *Tannenbaum* (Christmas tree) is one of the most important elements of a German Christmas – it's very rare that you will find an artificial tree in a German household. Many families don't decorate the tree until lunchtime on the 24th, making a real occasion of it. Usually there are candles, glass ornaments, orange slices, gingerbread cookies, *Lametta* (strips of silver to dangle from the tree, like icicles) and straw stars.

Heiligabend, the evening of Christmas Eve, is when *Bescherung*, the act of giving and receiving presents, takes place, and it's seen as sacred family time. Usually as dusk falls we put some festive music on – *Stille Nacht* ('Silent Night') is my favourite, and it brings a shiver down my spine to hear the angelic voices all around us as the candles on the tree are lit for the first time and the presents are shared.

For Germans *Heiligabend* is the pinnacle of Christmas, and as a child I felt very lucky starting our celebrations on the 24th knowing that everyone else in our little Welsh village had to wait until morning. Stockings on the 25th aren't commonplace in Germany, but for that German children have *Nikolaus* (see page 8) instead.

Usually there is a saucepan of mulled wine warming on the stovetop, which is continually topped up throughout the night, gently emitting a spiced fragrance into the already pine-scented room. It is one of the most delicious smells you could ever imagine, and along with flickering candlelight that dances about the room, the air is filled with magic and a generosity of spirit.

A favourite meal for Christmas Eve is *Kartoffelsalat mit Würstchen*, potato salad with sausages, though some families (ours included) choose to eat smoked fish in place of the sausages. Traditionally it was carp that was eaten on *Heiligabend* and my mum even remembers the Christmas carp swimming in the bathtub at home during the run-up, but I don't know anyone who still eats this. We personally choose to eat our potato salad at lunchtime and eat more of a relaxed *Abendbrot* in the evening, which consists of open sandwiches, crackers, cheese and pickles. The table is usually decorated with the *Adventskranz*, all four candles lit, and a *Weihnachtspyramide*, a wooden carousel with angels, shepherds and a manger all spinning gently inside a ring of candles. We don't eat a dessert as such, but I dot various *Bunte Teller* around the room for everyone to nibble at whenever they feel like.

The morning of the 25th is far more relaxed than it is in English-speaking countries and usually involves a leisurely breakfast that can go on till lunchtime, as family members lounge around the table and children play with toys they received the night before. The 25th and 26th are official holidays where extended family come over to feast and be merry. Usually a big lunch of roast goose with red cabbage and *Knödel* (potato dumplings) is eaten on the 25th with *Stollen* and coffee afterwards.

A family walk on the 26th seems to be a pretty universal thing. In Germany it's often the forest that people head to as a way to wind down the festivities and breath in the fresh air before the excitement of *Silvester* (New Year's Eve) begins.

Notes on baking and ingredients

SALT

I generally prefer not to specify exactly how much salt to use, so you should take the amounts given as a guide only. If it's a sweet biscuit recipe then a pinch will suffice, and for bread recipes I add anywhere between ¼ to 1½ teaspoons depending on whether or not it's a sweet or savoury bake. It's up to you how much you choose to put in, or not.

EGGS

All eggs are medium unless otherwise stated.

BUTTER

All butter is unsalted unless otherwise stated.

NUT GRINDING

I usually buy whole nuts and grind them at home using a coffee grinder; I find this best for keeping the nuts fresh, as you only need grind the required quantity.

MELTING CHOCOLATE

I add a little coconut oil to dark chocolate when melting it for coating bakes; this is because it prevents the chocolate from developing a white bloom if it hasn't been tempered.

YEAST

I prefer to use fresh yeast in my bakes as it ensures a much lighter texture in breads and yeasted doughs. It's definitely worth seeking out – you should be able to buy it from most bakeries. However, I have also given quantities for dried yeast if that's all you have to hand.

VANILLA SUGAR

This is a popular baking ingredient in Germany and is sold in little sachets alongside baking powder in the shops. I've generally chosen to use vanilla extract throughout the recipes in this book in place of the usual vanilla sugar as I feel it's more readily available outside of Germany, but should you have the strong kind of German vanilla sugar I'm talking about to hand then feel free to use a sachet (around 7g/¼oz) of that instead of the vanilla extract in each recipe. I have included vanilla sugar where it is sprinkled onto baked goods in a few recipes, but at a push caster (superfine) sugar will do.

BAKING SHEETS AND BATCH COOKING

Many of the biscuit and cookie recipes in this book require a couple or more large baking sheets. If you don't have enough in your kitchen, then baking in batches is always an option.

OVENS AND TIMINGS

I tested each of these recipes several times in my trusty domestic oven, in which I use the fan setting. Everyone's ovens are different – some run hotter than others, while some bake more slowly. I know my oven well, but I don't know yours. It's for this reason that I've often specified a window of baking times or given approximate timings. Always test to see if the bake is done at the earliest suggested time to avoid burning or drying out; keep baking a little longer if not quite done. And if your oven is temperamental or prone to an uneven bake, make sure to turn the sheet of biscuits or cake around halfway through cooking to ensure as even a bake as possible.

LEBKUCHENGEWÜRZ

A heady mixture of all the classic spices we might associate with Christmas time, and an essential ingredient for *Lebkuchen* and gingerbread-type biscuits (cookies). *Lebkuchengewürz* is readily available to buy throughout Germany but less easy to get hold of outside the country, which is why I've included a recipe for it on page 26.

POTTASCHE

Potash or potassium carbonate, as it's called in English, was around long before baking powder became popular as a leavener. While it isn't used extensively in baking today, it is still called for in a few specific traditional German Christmas biscuit recipes. You can find it easily enough online, but at a push it can be substituted with bicarbonate of soda (as I've done in the *Lebkuchen Allerlei* recipe on page 32).

RÜBENKRAUT

Rübenkraut is a sugar beet syrup, dark in colour and slightly thicker than a golden syrup or corn syrup. It is a popular condiment in Germany and often eaten on crisp bread rolls for breakfast as well as being an ingredient in baked goods. Its flavour is somewhere between treacle (molasses) and a date syrup. You can buy *Rübenkraut* online or in stores that specialize in German foods, but you can also substitute a mixture of date syrup and treacle in 3:1 proportions if you can't find it.

HIRSCHHORNSALZ

Baker's ammonia, or ammonium carbonate, in English, is a traditional raising agent used throughout Germany and Scandinavia for Christmas cookies. Many moons ago *Hirschhornsalz* was made out of ground deer antlers, hooves and horns, but these days it's chemically produced. Often used in butter-less biscuit dough, *Hirschhornsalz* gives cookies a unique tight-knit, crunchy texture — best described as a cross between a sponge cake and cinder toffee. It is a key ingredient in such biscuits as *Pfeffernüsse* and *Springerle*. While *Hirschhornsalz* is readily available to buy in little sachets all over Germany come Advent time, it is harder to get hold of elsewhere and you may need to order it online. I have known people to substitute *Hirschhornsalz* with an equal mixture of baking powder and bicarbonate of soda (baking soda), but personally I think it's worth seeking out and buying online should you not be able to find it in a local store.

Notes on the photographs

I took the majority of these photographs during lockdown, so wasn't able to have people over for lively parties and afternoons full of coffee and cake. Luckily we're a family of five at home and we bubbled with another young family as a support network, so I did manage to get some people into the photographs, though sadly not as many as I would have liked. All of the photographs were shot at home, except for a couple that I took at my friend Kelly's house.

Kelly has simple white walls (the perfect backdrop for food shots) around her kitchen table, in contrast to our kitchen walls, which are full of jars and pots. Shot in natural December light, most of the photographs were taken in the middle of the afternoon after a morning of baking, which is when Advent baked goods would most traditionally be eaten in Germany. Despite it not quite being dark at this time of day, candles are always lit to add a little warmth to the dwindling cold blue winter light.

Notes on the linocuts

The idea of 24 linocut illustrations (and so 24 chapters) is inspired by my love for old-fashioned Advent calendars, where a picture is revealed each day during the countdown to Christmas. I think there's something magical about these traditional paper calendars that modern chocolate versions fail to capture, and I had a wish to bring this same feeling alive in a book.

Working on the linocuts for this book was just the escape I needed from the monotony of lockdown (number three!). Walking into the studio (aka a bedroom with a pop-up desk by the window) each afternoon after a morning of home-schooling felt like stepping into another world, a world inspired by folk art and fairy tales. I lost myself in deep, dark woods, climbed up snowy mountains and strolled along the frosty pavements of Alpine towns. I skied down slopes and then sat by woodburning stoves with mugs of *Glühwein*, I gazed at snowflakes swirling outside the kitchen window and watched animals silently tiptoeing through the snow. I stood among resinous pine trees, breathing in deeply as night fell and fires were lit. And, of course, I baked in pretty, old-fashioned stoves and sat around candlelit tables with family and friends. This last vision, something I've always taken for granted up until now, is the thing I've yearned for the most over the past few months. All the baking I did while testing these recipes felt extra poignant, and I live in anticipation of Christmases shared to come.

I hope that my vision and images of winter depicted in the linocuts on these pages might transport you into another world or story too, and that you might find yourself travelling from your armchair, as I have, to break the spell of lockdown.

The 24 chapters of Advent

Salzteig

SALT DOUGH

Like most recipes, *Salzteig* is one that can be made at any time of year – far be it from me to dictate when you should make (and eat) anything. That said, making things out of salt dough is something we associate particularly with Christmas time, for it lends itself so well to tree decorations, candle holders, wreaths and festive ornaments.

We have spent countless afternoons together as a family making myriad different things out of salt dough. Favourites have included a multi-storey car park, woodland animals and a mini football pitch, all of which have been fun but somehow pale into comparison when it comes to the enjoyment and excitement to be had from making the *Adventskranz* (Advent wreath) each year.

The *Adventskranz* feels like the most important thing to come out of our oven. The phrase 'more than the sum of its parts' couldn't be truer than when referring to the centrepiece of our Advent table, around which we count down and build up Christmas. Lighting the candles, one during the first week, then two, three, four as the weeks add up, is a welcome ritual during the dark mornings and early nightfall of December.

Salt, flour and water is all you need for *Salzteig*. Beyond the ingredients and very simple method of making the actual dough, what you end up with will be entirely your own creation and it's a recipe you can let your imagination run wild with. There are no rules to follow, nothing to go wrong or worry about – it is, in every sense, child's play. And despite not being edible, this is one of the very first 'recipes' that many German children learn from their elders (or) at *Kindergarten*.

Salzteig
Salt dough

MAKES ENOUGH FOR A TABLE WREATH
OR A SET OF TREE DECORATIONS

*'Two cups of flour, one cup of salt and one cup of warm water,' Omi
(my maternal grandmother) would repeat gently as she clasped her
hand around mine, guiding me while we measured out the ingredients
using a coffee cup. This cup, chipped at the rim, redundant from
regular service and relegated to the ranks of 'measuring cup' is still in
my possession. Sitting on our kitchen shelf it reminds me that Salzteig
taught me how to feel my way around a recipe. That measurements
don't need to be exact for such simple things, just thereabouts, and that
the size of your cup is irrelevant; what counts is balancing proportions.*

2 cups plain
  (all-purpose) flour
1 cup table salt
1 cup warm water

Put the flour and salt into a large bowl and mix together. Pour the water into the centre and use your hands to mix the water in until a soft pliable dough is formed. Knead for a minute or two so that there are no lumps and the dough is nice and smooth.

Heat the oven to its lowest setting (my oven's lowest is 50°C/120°F).

Mould the dough as you would clay to form different objects. *Salzteig* rolls really well and is easy to cut out with cookie cutters – these make lovely tree decorations, just remember to make a hole for the string.

Once you've made your creations, place them on a baking sheet and pop them into the oven to dry out for 2 hours.

Remove the objects from the sheet and place on a wire rack to cool.

Once cool enough to handle, decorate as you wish with paint, glitter, varnish etc.

Lebkuchen

LEBKUCHEN

Lebkuchen, often described as 'German gingerbread' have to be the biscuit (cookie) most synonymous with Advent and German Christmases. They are without question the most traditional, and I'd argue most loved, of Advent bakes, stemming right back to the thirteenth century.

First baked by monks in Franconia, *Lebkuchen* were very basic, comprising of just honey, flour and spices. Historically, the dough was made at the end of October and rested in a cool spot until ready to bake in early December, as it was believed that the flavour and texture of the dough improved over time. The high proportion of honey acted not only as a sweetener but also as a 'preserver' during this long ripening period.

Over the last few hundred years, sugar, butter, nuts, eggs, candied peel and raising agents have all been introduced to the mix. One key traditional (but not medieval) ingredient, integral to *Lebkuchen*'s tight-knit texture, is *Pottasche* (potash or potassium carbonate), a precursor to baking powder. Unlike baking

powder, *Pottasche* doesn't leaven dough instantly. Instead it expands the dough slowly and requires a period of at least a couple of hours (and up to several weeks) to develop before baking.

Despite the use of *Pottasche* being ancient and possibly sounding a little strange compared to modern raising agents, traditional *Lebkuchen* aren't difficult to make at all; the test lies in patience.

Many spices can be included in *Lebkuchen* and I often think the general translation into English as 'gingerbread' is somewhat misleading. An authentic *Lebkuchengewürz* (*Lebkuchen* spice mix) comprises around seven spices and can include a combination of any of the following: ground cinnamon, ginger, cardamom, cloves, fennel, allspice, mace, nutmeg and anise. It's easy to make this mix yourself (and I've included a recipe for it in this chapter) but you can also buy it ready-made in little sachets.

Continued overleaf

Often, too, I take a shortcut and don't include every spice when baking *Lebkuchen* – it's not a deal breaker as far as I'm concerned, although I'm sure purists would disagree.

Most *Lebkuchen* have a dry crumb and are firm when first baked, which makes them an ideal dunking partner to a cup of tea or coffee. They will soften gradually over time though and will keep well if stored in an airtight container for weeks, if not months, on end. I actually prefer to eat them after a couple of days in the tin, allowing the spices time to settle in. Omi (my maternal grandmother) always popped a slice of apple into the tin alongside her *Lebkuchen* to speed up the softening process, and I've since learned that this wasn't a quirk personal to her, but is common practice among those who bake *Lebkuchen* at home. It is a habit I've now adopted too when storing *Honiglebkuchen, Lebkuchenherzen, Biberle* and *Mandelprinten*.

Many families have their own *Lebkuchen* recipe passed down from generation to generation in much the same way that a Christmas pudding recipe might be in the UK. I could have actually filled an entire book with variations of *Lebkuchen* recipes alone, but I've whittled the choice down to the six types I think best represent this magnificent biscuit, ranging from the old-fashioned *Pottasche*-leavened kind to the sort that are now commercially produced and sold in supermarkets across Germany and beyond. Each time I see a display of *Lebkuchen* and *Stollen* in UK supermarkets my heart skips a beat and I'm touched by how many people have adopted them as part of their regular Christmas celebrations. Now all we've got to do is convince Germany how good a mince pie is!

Lebkuchengewürz
Lebkuchen spice mix

MAKES ABOUT 8 TABLESPOONS

The flavour of this, and its scent, are 'quintessential Christmas'. For use in biscuits and cakes.

5 tbsp ground cinnamon
1 tbsp ground ginger
2 tsp ground cloves
1 tsp ground cardamom

1 tsp ground coriander
1 tsp ground anise
½ tsp ground mace

 ix all the ingredients thoroughly together in a bowl and store in an airtight jar for up to a year.

Elisenlebkuchen
Elisen Lebkuchen

MAKES 50 SMALL BISCUITS

Elisenlebkuchen stem from Nürnberg (Nuremberg), which lies in the heart of Franconia. When I stayed with my grandparents as a child we would take the train to this fairy-tale city during December to visit the magical Christkindlesmarkt and soak up the Advent spirit.

Soft, chewy and studded with candied peel, Elisenlebkuchen owe their texture to the use of ground nuts instead of flour. The biscuits are baked on Oblaten, little wheat or rice paper rounds, to prevent them from sticking to the baking sheet – it's believed that this method stems from monks originally using communion wafers.

Elisenlebkuchen come in a variety of shapes and sizes. Circular biscuits are most common, but rectangles or squares are fine too. The biscuits can be covered in chocolate or glazed with a thin sugar coating. I prefer the bite-sized round sugar-glazed version, which is what I've written a recipe for here. If you prefer them larger, simply use bigger Oblaten and lengthen the baking time by a couple of minutes.

2 eggs
180g (1 cup minus 1½ tbsp) soft light brown sugar
3 tbsp runny honey
175g (6oz) ground almonds (almond flour)
100g (⅘ cup) ground hazelnuts
½ tsp baking powder
125g (4oz) mixed peel, finely chopped
Finely grated zest of 1 orange
Finely grated zest of 1 lemon
2 tsp *Lebkuchengewürz* spice mix (see page 26) or 1½ tsp ground cinnamon mixed with ¼ tsp ground ginger and ¼ tsp ground cloves
Pinch of fine sea salt
50 × 5cm/2in diameter *Oblaten* (wheat or rice paper rounds)

FOR THE GLAZE
100g (scant ¾ cup) icing (confectioners') sugar, sifted
2 tbsp just-boiled water

Heat the oven to 160°C/140°C fan/320°F. Place all the ingredients, except for the *Oblaten*, in a large mixing bowl. Using a wooden spoon, mix until a rough, craggy dough is formed, at which point start beating more vigorously until the dough is as smooth as possible (bearing in mind it will have lumps because of the candied peel). The dough will be quite tacky.

Divide the *Oblaten* between two large baking sheets. (These don't spread much and so I don't feel the need to line the baking sheets with parchment, but there's no harm in doing so if you choose to play it on the safe side.)

Spoon a heaped teaspoon of dough onto each *Oblate* and, using the back of the spoon, spread it gently down until it's a couple of millimetres (¹⁄₁₆in) shy of the paper edges.

Bake in the oven for about 20 minutes until just golden and firm to the touch. During the last 5 minutes of baking time, mix the icing sugar with the just-boiled water until a smooth, glossy icing is formed. Remove the biscuits from the oven and transfer to a wire rack immediately. Work quickly to brush each *Lebkuchen* with the glaze. Allow the biscuits to cool and make sure the icing is dry before storing in an airtight tin or jar. They will keep for well over a month if stored correctly.

If you choose to cover the biscuits with chocolate instead, follow the same method as per the biscuits on page 118.

Pictured overleaf

Lebkuchenherzen
Lebkuchen hearts

These Lebkuchen are very easy to make and are the type of recipe that many German households bake in the run-up to Christmas. Hearts are the most popular shape, but stars, Christmas trees, angels and bells all add a festive touch.

I use both flour and ground nuts in this recipe, making these a cross between Elisenlebkuchen and a traditional spiced honey version. These biscuits are quite sweet owing to the addition of brown sugar, and I feel a frosting would tip the balance over the edge, so I've opted simply to decorate them in the traditional manner with blanched almonds and cherries.

120g (⅓ cup minus 1 tbsp) runny honey
120g (⅔ cup minus 1 tbsp) dark brown sugar
65g (4½ tbsp) unsalted butter
115g (1 cup minus 1 tbsp) plain (all-purpose) flour, plus extra for dusting
115g (1 cup plus ½ tbsp) rye flour
75g (⅔ cup) ground almonds (almond flour)
1 egg
2½ tsp *Lebkuchen-gewürz* (see page 26) or 1 tsp ground cinnamon mixed with 1 tsp ground ginger, ¼ tsp ground cloves and ¼ tsp ground cardamom
½ tbsp unsweetened cocoa powder
½ tsp bicarbonate of soda (baking soda)
30g (1oz) mixed peel, finely chopped
Finely grated zest of ½ lemon
Pinch of fine sea salt

TO DECORATE
1 egg white, loosened with a fork
15 blanched almonds
5 glacé cherries, quartered

eat the honey, sugar and butter in a small saucepan over a gentle heat, until melted and blended together, stirring from time to time to avoid sticking. Set aside.

Put the remaining ingredients into a large mixing bowl, pour over the melted honey mixture and stir everything together with a wooden spoon until a sticky dough is formed. Cover the bowl with a tea towel and set aside for 1 hour – it will become much less sticky and easier to work with after this rest.

Heat the oven to 180°C/160°C fan/350°F. Line two baking sheets with non-stick baking parchment.

Roll out the dough on a lightly floured surface to a 5mm/⅛in thickness. Using a heart-shaped cookie cutter (see pages 258–9), stamp out hearts and place them 2cm/¾in apart on the prepared sheets. Re-roll the dough offcuts into more biscuits. Brush the top of each heart with egg white and place either an almond or a cherry quarter in the centre of each.

Bake in the oven for 12–15 minutes until golden brown and just firm to the touch. Allow to cool on the sheet for a few minutes before transferring to a wire rack to cool completely. Store in an airtight container, where they will keep for a month or more. (I add a slice of apple to sit in the tin alongside these to help them soften quickly and stay soft, but they will soften gradually without the help of the apple too. It all boils down to whether or not you like a hard cookie or a soft one.)

Pictured overleaf

Lebkuchen Allerlei
Lebkuchen allsorts

MAKES ABOUT 40, DEPENDING ON SHAPE

I based this recipe on traditional honey Lebkuchen but instead of using Pottasche as a leavener I use bicarbonate of soda, which gives a slightly looser-textured, more airy biscuit that becomes pleasantly chewy as it softens and matures in the tin over time. The rye flour gives these biscuits a distinct nutty flavour without making the dough dense.

These can be made into any shape, hence their name — hearts and circles are both common.

50g (3½ tbsp) unsalted butter
250g (¾ cup) runny honey
125g (1 cup plus 2 tbsp) rye flour
100g (¾ cup) plain (all-purpose) flour, plus extra for dusting
1 tsp bicarbonate of soda (baking soda)
1 tbsp *Lebkuchen-gewürz* spice mix (see page 26) or 1½ tsp ground cinnamon mixed with 1 tsp ground ginger and ½ tsp ground cloves
1 tsp unsweetened cocoa powder
Pinch of fine sea salt

FOR THE ICING
200g (scant 1½ cups) icing (confectioners') sugar, sifted
1 large egg white (if you're worried about using raw egg white you can use 2 tbsp water instead, but trust me, egg is better)
Pink food colouring (optional)
Sprinkles (optional)

Melt the butter and honey in a saucepan over a low heat for a few minutes, stirring until the butter has melted and is incorporated into the honey. Allow to cool.

Put all the dry ingredients into a large bowl, pour over the buttery honey and mix vigorously until tacky and dense. Cover the bowl with a tea towel and set aside to rest for anywhere between 3 and 8 hours (overnight is ideal). At this point the dough might seem unworkable, but after resting it firms up and becomes pliable.

Heat the oven to 200°C/180°C fan/400°F. Line two baking sheets with non-stick baking parchment.

Divide the dough into four equal parts and, on a floured surface, gently roll each into a sausage shape about 1cm/⅜in in diameter. Using a sharp knife, cut the sausages into 5cm/2in lengths and place them on the sheets, leaving 4cm/1½in of space between each, as these do tend to spread.

Bake for about 8 minutes until dry to the touch and no longer tacky.

While the biscuits are baking, mix the icing sugar and egg white together in a bowl until smooth. If you like, add a couple of drops of food colouring and stir through.

Take the biscuits out of the oven and allow to cool for a few minutes before transferring to a wire rack. While still warm, spoon a teaspoon of icing along each biscuit. The icing should be liquid enough to start slowly running over the biscuit — if some areas aren't covered, give it a helping hand by spreading with a spatula or knife. If using sprinkles, scatter some over the biscuits at this point before the icing sets.

Leave to dry for a couple of hours until the icing is set, then store the biscuits in an airtight container. They will soften naturally over time and keep well in the tin for up to 3 weeks.

Gefüllte Lebkuchenherzen
Jam-filled Lebkuchen hearts

These little Lebkuchen hearts give way to a soft interior of jam. They are traditionally filled with Pflaumenmus (a spiced plum butter) but any sharp, smooth jam – redcurrant jelly, damson jelly, sour cherry jam (sieved) – will all work really well.

At first, these Lebkuchen seem slightly fiddly to make, but if you like them enough to make a second batch, which I'm hoping is the case, you'll soon realize once you've got the hang of it that there's actually not much to it.

50g (3½ tbsp) unsalted butter
200g (½ cup plus 1½ tbsp) runny honey
125g (1 cup minus ½ tbsp) plain (all-purpose) flour, plus extra for dusting
125g (1 cup plus 2 tbsp) rye flour
1 tsp bicarbonate of soda (baking soda)
1 tbsp *Lebkuchen-gewürz* spice mix (see page 26) or 1 tsp ground ginger

mixed with 1½ tsp ground cinnamon and ½ tsp ground cloves
Pinch of fine sea salt
25g (1oz) mixed peel, very finely chopped

FOR THE FILLING
80g (3oz) jam (jelly)

FOR THE GLAZE
6 tbsp icing (confectioners') sugar, sifted
1 tbsp just-boiled water
1½ tsp lemon juice

Melt the butter and honey in a saucepan over a low heat for a few minutes, stirring until the butter has melted and is incorporated into the honey. Allow to cool.

Heat the oven to 180°C/160°C fan/350°F.

Put the dry ingredients and mixed peel into a bowl, pour over the honey mixture and stir everything together. When it becomes too difficult to stir, use your hands to bring the mixture together into a dough, then knead for a few minutes until smooth.

Split the dough in half. Roll out one half on a lightly floured surface to around 3mm/⅛in thick. Using a heart-shaped cookie cutter (see pages 258–9), cut out 10 hearts and place them on a large baking sheet (or two small), spaced about 2cm/¾in apart. Spoon ½ teaspoon of jam onto the centre of each heart.

Now roll out the other half of the dough to the same thickness and cut out 10 more hearts. Roll over them again so that they become slightly larger and thinner (as they need to be domed over the jam).

Dip your finger into a bowl of water and run it around the dough edge of the jam-covered hearts. Place the larger hearts on top and seal the edges by pressing round them lightly with your fingertips. Re-roll all the dough offcuts into more biscuits.

Bake in the centre of the oven for about 12 minutes until slightly golden and firm to the touch, but not browned or hard.

While the biscuits are baking, mix all the glaze ingredients together in a bowl to a smooth icing.

Transfer the biscuits to a wire rack and, while still warm, brush the tops with the glaze. Allow to cool fully before transferring to an airtight container. They will keep well for a month.

Also pictured: Nussstangen *(p.128),* Schwarz-Weiß Gebäck *(p.138)*

Honiglebkuchen
Old-fashioned honey Lebkuchen

MAKES ABOUT 25

If you are used to the flavour and consistency of modern commercial Lebkuchen, be warned this recipe might not be what you expect from a biscuit of the same name.

This is as close to an old-fashioned traditional Lebkuchen recipe as I can get and I've included it here both because of this and because I find it interesting to see how tastes and methods have changed over centuries.

During the development of the recipe I made several batches, which my mum tasted (with eyes closed) to let me know if they resembled those Lebkuchen of her childhood (just to clarify, Mama isn't hundreds of years old, but she's the closest, most reliable taste tester I have going back many decades).

These biscuits have a unique texture and springiness about them owing to the use of Pottasche as a leavener; they also aren't as sweet as many modern versions. But the one thing that is probably universally obvious and recognizable about them is that they are the biscuits that make up the wicked witch's house in the Grimm's fairy tale Hänsel und Gretel.

250g (¾ cup) runny honey
50g (3½ tbsp) unsalted butter
1 tsp *Pottasche* (see page 13)
1 tbsp water
125g (1 cup minus ½ tbsp) plain (all-purpose) flour, plus extra for dusting
125g (1 cup plus 2 tbsp) rye flour
1 small egg
1 tbsp *Lebkuchen-gewürz* spice mix (see page 26) or 1½ tsp ground cinnamon mixed with 1 tsp ground ginger and ½ tsp ground cloves
2 tsp unsweetened cocoa powder
80g (3oz) mixed peel, finely chopped
Finely grated zest of 1 lemon

TO DECORATE
1 egg white, loosened with a fork
Glacé cherries, halved
Blanched almonds

Melt the honey and the butter in a saucepan over a low heat, stirring until the butter is absorbed into the honey. Allow to cool. In a small glass, dissolve the *Pottasche* with the water.

Put the rest of the dough ingredients into a large mixing bowl, then pour over the honey mixture followed by the dissolved *Pottasche*. Beat vigorously with a wooden spoon until a tacky, dense dough forms.

Cover the bowl tightly with a tea towel and set aside for at least 24 hours – and up to 6 weeks. The longest I've rested my dough is 2 weeks, but apparently the longer you leave it the better it is. Usually, though, I only rest mine for 24 hours.

Heat the oven to 200°C/180°C fan/400°F. Line two baking sheets with non-stick baking parchment.

Roll out the dough on a lightly floured surface to about 8mm/¼in thick. Using a sharp knife, cut out rectangles of around 4 × 7cm (1½ × 2¾in) – they don't need to be exact, in fact I quite like the patchwork of different sizes on a plate.

Gently place the biscuits on the two sheets, leaving 3cm/1¼in between each to allow for spreading. Brush the top of each with egg white then decorate with cherries and almonds.

Bake for 8–10 minutes until firm to the touch but not browned. Transfer to a wire rack. Once cool, store in an airtight tin, for up to 6 weeks.

Mandelprinten
Spiced almond Lebkuchen

MAKES ABOUT 30

Aachener Printen are a particular type of Lebkuchen that, no surprises here, stem from the German city of Aachen. They are protected by a PDO (protected design of origin), meaning that only biscuits produced within and around the city limits can be called Aachener Printen. Dotted around the city, each of the bakeries boasts its own unique version.

Originally, hundreds of years ago, the biscuits were made with honey, but over time the honey has been substituted with Rübenkraut (sugar beet syrup), which is what gives them their signature flavour. Rübenkraut is dark in colour and has a taste and consistency akin to treacle but it is sweeter and much less bitter, possibly closer to date molasses.

I think Aachener Printen are one of the finest Lebkuchen varieties around and my love for them led to a family pilgrimage to Aachen during December 2017, where we spent two frosty days wide-eyed with wonder, admiring several bakehouse window displays and eating our way through as many variations as possible. I think the mystery surrounding the closely guarded recipes and the city limit constrictions of this biscuit are all part of the Printen's charm. These are my take on my favourite almond variety.

75g (⅓ cup) unsalted butter

200g (½ cup plus 1½ tbsp) *Rübenkraut* or, if you can't get hold of any, then use 50g (2½ tbsp) treacle and 150g (½ cup minus 1 tbsp) runny honey instead

50g (¼ cup) dark brown sugar

1 tsp *Pottasche* (see page 13)

1 tbsp water

50g (½ cup minus 1 tbsp) rye flour

175g (1⅓ cups) plain (all-purpose) flour, plus extra for dusting

40g (1½oz) flaked (slivered) almonds, roughly chopped

2 tsp *Lebkuchengewürz* spice mix (see page 26) or 1 tsp ground cinnamon mixed with ½ tsp ground ginger, ¼ tsp ground cloves and ¼ tsp ground anise

1 tsp unsweetened cocoa powder

Pinch of fine sea salt

TO DECORATE

100g (3½oz) blanched almonds, roughly chopped

Melt the butter, *Rübenkraut* and brown sugar together in a saucepan over a low heat until the sugar has dissolved into the liquid. Allow to cool. In a small glass, dissolve the *Pottasche* in the water.

Put all the dry ingredients into a large bowl, then pour in the butter mixture followed by the dissolved *Pottasche*. Beat with a wooden spoon until a tacky, dense dough is formed. It will seem unworkable at this stage but will firm up over time. Cover the bowl with a tea towel and set aside to rest for 3–8 hours (overnight is ideal).

Heat the oven to 180°C/160°C fan/350°F. Line two baking sheets with non-stick baking parchment.

Roll out the dough on a lightly floured surface to 1cm/⅜in thick. Using a sharp knife, cut out little rectangles, about 2.5 × 5cm (1 × 2in).

Place the chopped almonds in a dish and, one at a time, very gently press each biscuit into the dish, so the almonds stick, flip the biscuit over and repeat to cover both sides. Place the biscuits 3cm/1¼in apart on the lined sheets.

Bake for 10–12 minutes until firm but not browned. Allow to cool for a couple of minutes before transferring to a wire rack. Once cool, store in an airtight container. These will last for over a month and soften gradually over time.

3

Adventsfrühstück

ADVENT BREAKFAST

Breakfast in Germany on a weekday is much the same as it is in many European countries, nothing glamorous, just a simple slice of bread or toast spread with jam or a bowl of cereal before rushing out of the door. At the weekend, this morning ritual changes unrecognizably into – I'll lay my hat on the line here – what I believe to be the finest breakfast the world has to offer.

A weekend *Frühstück* is a relaxed affair, which may well take up the best part of a day, but without all the pretence that surrounds a 'brunch'. I've never been a fan of brunch and what the word encompasses, which is to blend two great things – breakfast and lunch – into one; I just don't see the point of compressing pleasure. Why enjoy once what you could have twice over? Or, as is the case with *Frühstück*, simply roll on one from the other which, let me be clear, is not the same as making them one.

Frühstück at the weekend is a veritable feast of various rolls/breads, sweet condiments (jams, honey, preserves, chocolate spread), cheeses (including and possibly most importantly *Quark*), patés and cold cured meats, sausages, eggs, fruit, light salads (often just sliced tomato

and cucumber), yogurt, fruit juice, coffee, tea and cocoa – all laid out effortlessly. I say effortlessly because aside from boiling some eggs and heating water for hot drinks there is no cooking involved at all, unless you choose to make your own bread rolls, which might take a little effort, yes, but is in fact just pleasure disguised.

Adventsfrühstück is eaten on the four Sundays in the run-up to Christmas as we count down the days, bathed in warm candlelight around a wreath at the centre of the table. Inviting friends over to share in this celebration is the epitome of *Gemütlichkeit* (cosiness). Baking and Advent go hand in hand, and while biscuits (cookies) are the traditional offering when friends come over, I don't know of a more welcoming way to invite anyone in from the cold than to open up the front door to a house that smells of freshly baked bread.

The last thing anyone wants during the festive season is to feel under pressure by having to put on an amazing spread – I've written all the recipes in this chapter with this in mind, so they can be prepared the night before with minimum effort on the morning of your *Adventsfrühstück*.

Müslibrötchen
Muesli breakfast rolls

MAKES 10

These rolls are perfect for Frühstück's *array of sweet and savoury toppings, as dried fruit in the muesli pairs well with both jam and cheese. These keep well for a day or two and filled with cheese make a refreshing change to a lunch box sandwich. Our favourite way to eat them for breakfast is a classic German way – a thick layer of creamy* Quark *followed by a dollop of jam.*

320ml (1⅓ cups) whole milk
2 tbsp runny honey
15g (½oz) fresh yeast, or 7g (¼oz) dried
450g (3¼ cups) strong white bread flour (or 50/50 white and wholemeal/wholewheat), plus extra for dusting
100g (3½oz) muesli, plus a handful for the tops
1½ tsp fine sea salt

In a small saucepan, gently heat the milk and honey for a couple of minutes until tepid. Take off the heat and add the yeast, whisking until it has dissolved.

Mix the flour, muesli and salt in a large bowl. Pour in the yeasted milk and, using your hands, bring everything together until a rough dough is formed. Tip the dough out onto a floured surface and knead for 10 minutes until it becomes more elastic. Form it into a neat ball and nestle it into the bottom of the bowl. Cover the bowl with a tea towel and set aside in a warm spot to rise for about 1 hour, or until doubled in size. (Alternatively, add the ingredients as directed above to the bowl of a free-standing electric mixer fitted with a dough hook, and knead for 5 minutes until elastic. Cover the bowl and set aside, as above.)

If baking the rolls now, heat the oven to 220°C/200°C fan/430°F and line a large baking sheet with non-stick baking parchment. If baking the rolls the next day you will need to line two smaller sheets, as a large one won't fit in the fridge.

Knock the dough back with your fist, tip out onto the work surface and, using a bread scraper or sharp knife, split it into 10 equal pieces. With wet hands, form each piece into a bun by pulling the sides down and tucking them into the bottom of the dough. Now hold each bun in turn in one hand while you pinch and pull two opposite ends with your free hand to create an almond-shaped roll.

Place the rolls on the prepared baking sheet and let them rest, covered, until risen to half their size again – this usually takes 30 minutes in a warm place (I keep them on top of the stove while the oven is heating up below), but may take longer depending on the temperature of your kitchen. If you are baking the rolls in the morning, arrange them on two smaller sheets, place in the fridge, covered, and let them rise overnight. Take the rolls out of the fridge 20 minutes before baking.

Brush the tops of the risen rolls with water and sprinkle over some muesli. Using a serrated knife, cut down into each roll lengthwise from one pointed end to the other. It's important to make the cut deep (at least 2cm/¾in) so the roll splits open sufficiently when baked.

Bake for 12–15 minutes until golden brown. Tap the base of one of the rolls with your knuckles; if it sounds hollow it is done. A dull sound indicates the dough is still too dense and they will need another couple of minutes in the oven.

Transfer the rolls onto a wire rack to cool. Best served warm or shortly after they're baked.

Brötchen mit Kürbiskernen
Seeded rye rolls

MAKES 10

Usually seeded rolls in Germany contain an array of seeds such as linseed, poppy and sesame, and have a particularly nutty flavour. But the bakery local to my grandparent's house in Bavaria used to specialize in a pumpkin seed variety. Pumpkin seeds are very popular in bread baking throughout Austria and Germany and as well as adding a creamy, earthy flavour and texture, they brighten the Advent table with their festive leafy green colour.

300g (2 cups plus 2 tbsp) strong white bread flour, plus extra for dusting
150g (1⅓ cups) rye flour
1½ tsp fine sea salt

15g (½oz) fresh yeast, or 7g (¼oz) dried
300ml (1¼ cups) tepid water
75g (2½oz) pumpkin or sunflower seeds (or a mixture)

Mix both flours and the salt together in a large bowl. Crumble the yeast (or sprinkle if using dried) into the tepid water and stir to dissolve. Pour the yeasted water into the flour mixture and, using your hands, bring everything together until a rough dough is formed. Tip the dough out onto a lightly floured work surface and knead for about 10 minutes until it becomes more elastic. Form it into a ball and nestle it into the bottom of the bowl. Cover the bowl with a tea towel and set aside in a warm spot to rise for about 1 hour, or until doubled in size. (Alternatively, put both flours and the salt into the bowl of a free-standing electric mixer, pour in the yeasted water and, using a dough hook, knead for 5 minutes until the dough is elastic. Cover the bowl and set aside, as above.)

Put the seeds into a shallow dish.

If baking the rolls now, heat the oven to 220°C/200°C fan/430°F and line a large baking sheet with non-stick baking parchment. If baking the rolls the next day you will need to line two smaller sheets, as a large one won't fit in the fridge.

Knock the dough back with your fist, tip out onto the work surface and, using a bread scraper or sharp knife split it into 10 equal pieces. With wet hands, form each piece into a bun by pulling the sides down and tucking them under the dough. Dip each roll into the dish of seeds so that they stick. Now hold each bun in turn in one hand while you pinch and pull two opposite ends with your free hand to create an almond-shaped roll.

Place the rolls on the prepared baking sheet and let them rest, covered, until risen to half their size again – this usually takes 30 minutes in a warm place (I keep them on top of the stove while the oven is heating up below), but may take longer depending on the temperature of your kitchen. If you are baking your rolls in the morning, arrange them on two smaller sheets, place in the fridge, covered, and let them rise overnight. Take the rolls out of the fridge 20 minutes before baking.

Using a serrated knife, cut down into each roll lengthwise from one pointed end to the other. It's important to make the cut deep (at least 2cm/¾in) so the roll splits open sufficiently when baked.

Bake for 12–15 minutes until golden brown. Tap the base of one of the rolls with your knuckles; if it sounds hollow it is done. A dull sound indicates the dough is still too dense and they will need another couple of minutes in the oven.

Transfer the rolls onto a wire rack to cool. Best served warm or shortly after they're baked.

Käsebrötchen mit Mohn
Cheese and poppy seed rolls

MAKES 10

The beauty of these rolls lies in the fact that they are complete in themselves and therefore brilliant for lunch boxes and picnics. This recipe is an idea that has evolved from a beloved German Schwarzwälderschinken (Black forest ham) and cheese Pretzel roll which I love to eat cut in half and layered with cold slabs of unsalted butter.

This dough isn't based on a Pretzel though, as truth be told I find Pretzels hard to master, but instead is based on the archetypal German Brötchen, made out of a simple wheat flour yeasted dough.

450g (3¼ cups) strong white bread flour, plus extra for dusting
10g (⅓oz) poppy seeds, plus extra for sprinkling
1½ tsp fine sea salt

15g (½oz) fresh yeast, or 7g (¼oz) dried
290ml (1¼ cups minus 2 tsp) tepid water
100g (3½oz) Emmental or mature Cheddar, grated

ix the flour, poppy seeds and salt in a large bowl. Crumble the yeast (or sprinkle if using dried) into the tepid water and stir to dissolve. Pour the yeasted water into the flour mixture and, using your hands, bring everything together until a rough dough is formed. Tip the dough out onto a floured surface and knead for about 10 minutes until it becomes more elastic. Form it into a ball and nestle it back into the bottom of the bowl. Cover the bowl with a tea towel and set aside in a warm spot to rise for about 1 hour, or until doubled in size. (Alternatively, put the flour, poppy seeds and salt into the bowl of a free-standing electric mixer fitted with a dough hook, pour in the yeasted water and knead for 5 minutes until the dough is elastic. Cover the bowl and set aside, as above.)

If baking the rolls now, heat the oven to 220°C/200°C fan/430°F and line a large baking sheet with non-stick baking parchment. If baking the rolls the next day you will need to line two smaller sheets, as a large one won't fit in the fridge.

Knock the dough back with your fist, tip out onto the work surface and, using a bread scraper or sharp knife split it into 10 equal pieces. With wet hands, form each piece into a bun by pulling the sides down and tucking them under the dough. Now hold each bun in turn in one hand while you pinch and pull two opposite ends with your free hand to create an almond-shaped roll.

Place the rolls on the prepared sheet and let them rest, covered, until risen to half their size – this usually takes 30 minutes in a warm place, but may take longer depending on the temperature of your kitchen. If baking the rolls in the morning, arrange on two smaller sheets, place in the fridge, covered, and let them rise overnight. Take the rolls out of the fridge 20 minutes before baking.

Using a serrated knife, cut down into each roll lengthwise from one pointed end to the other. It's important to make the cut deep (at least 2cm/¾in) so the roll splits open sufficiently when baked.

Bake for 6 minutes before topping each roll with cheese and a sprinkling of poppy seeds. Return them to the oven for 8–10 minutes. Tap the base of one of the rolls with your knuckles; if it sounds hollow it is done. A dull sound indicates the dough is still too dense and they will need another couple of minutes in the oven.

Transfer the rolls onto a wire rack to cool. Best served warm or shortly after they're baked.

Gewürzbrötchen
Spiced rye rolls

MAKES 10

These rolls are a typical Roggenmischbrot, *which is basically a bread dough made with wheat and rye flours usually flavoured with* Brotgewürz, *a spice mix that includes coriander, fennel, anise seeds and caraway. You can buy the spice mix in little sachets but I prefer it unground, adding little pops of flavour to each bite. Bread spiced with* Brotgewürz *is an acquired taste, particularly where children are concerned. As a child I thought it tasted of cough syrup and it was my least favourite type of bread, but nowadays the haunting liquorice flavours of anise and fennel alongside the musty citrus edge of coriander and caraway are a comforting taste of home.*

350g (2½ cups) strong white bread flour, plus extra for dusting
100g (1 cup minus 1 tbsp) rye flour (or wholemeal/wholewheat)
½ tsp coriander seeds
½ tsp fennel seeds
½ tsp anise seeds
½ tsp caraway seeds
1½ tsp fine sea salt
15g (½oz) fresh yeast, or 7g (¼oz) dried
300ml (1¼ cups) tepid water

Mix the flour, spices and salt in a large bowl. Crumble the yeast (or sprinkle if using dried) into the tepid water and stir to dissolve. Pour the yeasted water into the flour mixture and, using your hands, bring everything together until a rough dough is formed. Tip out onto a floured surface and knead for 10 minutes until it becomes elastic. Form it into a ball and nestle it into the bottom of the bowl. Cover the bowl with a tea towel and set aside in a warm spot to rise for 1 hour, or until doubled in size. (Alternatively, put the flour, spices and salt into the bowl of a free-standing electric mixer fitted with a dough hook, add the yeasted water and knead for 5 minutes until elastic. Cover the bowl and set aside, as above.)

If baking the rolls now, heat the oven to 220°C/200°C fan/430°F and line a large baking sheet with non-stick baking parchment. If baking the rolls the next day you will need to line two smaller sheets, as a large one won't fit in the fridge.

Knock the dough back with your fist, tip out onto the work surface and, using a bread scraper or sharp knife, split it into 10 pieces of roughly the same size. Wet your hands and form each piece into a bun by pulling the sides down and tucking them into the bottom of the dough. Now hold each bun in turn in one hand while you pinch and pull two opposite ends with your free hand to create an almond-shaped roll.

Place the rolls on the prepared sheet and let them rest, covered, until risen to half their size – this usually takes 30 minutes in a warm place, but may take longer depending on the temperature of your kitchen. If baking the rolls in the morning, arrange on two smaller sheets, place in the fridge, covered, and let them rise overnight. Take the rolls out of the fridge 20 minutes before baking.

Using a serrated knife, cut down into each roll lengthwise from one pointed end to the other. It's important to make the cut deep (at least 2cm/¾in) so the roll splits open sufficiently when baked.

Bake for 12–15 minutes until golden brown. Tap the base of one of the rolls with your knuckles; if it sounds hollow it is done. A dull sound indicates the dough is still too dense and they will need another couple of minutes in the oven.

Transfer the rolls onto a wire rack to cool. Best served warm or shortly after they're baked.

Mohnschnecken
Poppy seed snails

MAKES 10 SMALL SNAILS

Poppy seeds have a particular nutty depth of flavour to them, which I find terribly hard to describe because there isn't anything else like it. They are used in baking year round in many Northern European countries, but it's during Advent and Christmas that they really come into their own, as they are an integral ingredient to many enriched yeast dough bakes such as Mohnstollen (poppy seed Stollen) on page 93 and these delicious little buns.

300g (2 cups plus 2 tbsp) strong white bread flour, plus extra for dusting
20g (4 tsp) caster (superfine) sugar
½ tsp fine sea salt
50g (3½ tbsp) unsalted butter, at room temp
15g (½oz) fresh yeast, or 7g (¼oz) dried
170ml (⅔ cup) tepid milk

FOR THE FILLING
80g (3oz) poppy seeds, ground (I use a coffee grinder)
80g (3oz) raisins
50g (¼ cup) dark brown sugar
85ml (6 tbsp) hot milk

FOR THE TOP
Milk, for brushing
Poppy seeds, for sprinkling

FOR THE GLAZE
80g (generous ½ cup) icing (confectioners') sugar, sifted
4 tsp water

 o make the filling put the poppy seeds, raisins and sugar into a bowl and pour over the hot milk. Set aside until cool, then stir.

Mix the flour, sugar and salt in a large bowl. Using your fingertips, work the butter into the flour until it resembles fine breadcrumbs. Crumble the yeast (or sprinkle if using dried) into the tepid milk and stir to dissolve. Pour the yeasted milk into the flour mixture and, using your hands, bring everything together into a rough dough. Tip out onto a floured surface and knead for 5 minutes until it becomes elastic.

Form it into a ball and nestle it into the bowl. Cover the bowl with a tea towel and set aside in a warm spot to rise for 1 hour, or until doubled in size. (Alternatively, mix the flour, sugar and salt in the bowl of a free-standing electric mixer fitted with a dough hook, then add the butter and yeasted milk. Knead for 5 minutes until elastic. Cover the bowl and set aside, as above.)

Line a medium baking sheet with non-stick baking parchment. Knock the dough back, then roll it out on a floured surface into a rectangle 30cm/12in long by 20cm/8in wide. Spread the poppy seed filling over the dough, leaving a 1cm/⅜in border. Dip your finger in water and run it around the edges. With the long side closest to you, roll the dough up into a log. Cut the dough into 10 rounds, about 3cm/1¼in thick. Place 3cm/1¼in apart on the prepared baking sheet.

If baking now, heat the oven to 180°C/160°C fan/350°F. Let them rest until risen to half their size again – this should take 30 minutes. If baking in the morning, place the sheet, covered, in the fridge to rest overnight, making sure you take them out of the fridge 30 minutes before baking.

Brush the snails with milk, sprinkle with poppy seeds, and bake for about 15 minutes until golden.

While they are baking, make the glaze by mixing the icing sugar and water together until smooth.

Transfer the baked snails to a wire rack and spoon the glaze over the top of them while still warm.

4

Zwieback und Biscotti

TWICE BAKED BISCUITS

Zwieback (directly translated as twice baked) are one of the first biscuits (cookies) children in Germany eat. They are particularly dry and crunchy due to the double bake and you'll often see teething babies and toddlers in pushchairs clinging onto one with a chubby fist. Often, too, for toddler snacks or breakfast at home a *Zwieback* is placed in a shallow bowl onto which warm milk is poured, then left to stand for a minute or so, by which time the *Zwieback* has soaked up all the milk like a sponge and can be mushed with a spoon into an instant porridge.

These sort of *Zwieback* aren't traditionally Christmas biscuits, they're just simple German biscuits. But there is nothing to say they can't be part of Advent baking, and once spices, nuts and dried fruit are added to a *Zwieback* dough they become altogether festive. I first ate such a *Zwieback* (of the walnut and cinnamon variety) on a *Bunter Teller* passed across the garden fence from Omi's (my maternal grandmother) neighbour Anni. Anni kept things simple, she was austere in nature, and it came across in everything she did — her *Bunter Teller* was not very *bunt* (colourful), in fact it was positively

brown. She stuck to what she knew and what was good; why add sprinkles and glitzy icing? And she had a point. While not fully aligned with her way of thinking, I do think a *Bunter Teller* should be built around the classics, but with a little room for new or modern additions too.

And on that note, I should probably mention that I add not typically German — actually very Italian — *Biscotti* to my plate because Germany is where I first ate them. Nearly every Bavarian town (I'm sure this is true for towns up and down the country) has an Italian ice-cream parlour, where strong coffee and *Biscotti* are served alongside balls of the most delectable *Gelati*. What *Biscotti* and *Zwieback* have in common is that they are both twice baked. The main, and pretty much only difference as far as I can see, is that *Biscotti* are made with whole eggs, while *Zwieback* use only the white.

Whether it's Advent or not, our house is never without a jar of *Zwieback* or *Biscotti* on the shelf. And while not novel in the same way that seasonal treats are, *Zwieback* have a firm spot on our *Bunter Teller* and add a touch of calm familiarity among all the Christmas hype.

Walnusszwieback
Walnut and cinnamon rusks

MAKES ABOUT 30

*Because these contain no butter and are twice baked, creating
a crisp, dry biscuit, they keep for an exceptionally long time,
qualifying them as one of the first bakes on my Advent list.*

3 egg whites
80g (½ cup minus
1 tbsp) caster
(superfine) sugar
125g (1 cup minus
1 tbsp) plain
(all-purpose) flour

1 tsp ground cinnamon
Pinch of fine sea salt
125g (4oz) walnuts,
roughly chopped

Heat the oven to 180°C/160°C fan/350°F and line a 450g (1lb) loaf tin (pan) with non-stick baking parchment that hangs substantially over the edges (this is important because the loaf will be wrapped up in this parchment before the second bake).

Put the egg whites into the bowl of a free-standing electric mixer (or in a large bowl using a hand-held electric whisk) and whisk on high speed until stiff peaks form. Reduce the speed of the whisk slightly and add the sugar, one tablespoon at a time, whisking all the while, until it's all incorporated and has turned into a glossy meringue.

Mix the flour, cinnamon, salt and chopped walnuts together in a separate bowl. Add half the flour mixture to the meringue mixture and, using a large metal spoon, fold it through gently. Now add the remaining flour mixture and do the same, trying to knock as little air out as possible.

Gently spoon the mixture into the prepared loaf tin, levelling the top as best you can with the back of the spoon.

Bake in the oven for 25–30 minutes, until firm to the touch and only just starting to turn golden brown. Lift it out gently onto a wire rack with the parchment still attached. Allow to cool completely before wrapping the parchment around it so that it's sealed. Leave to sit for 5 hours (or overnight) – this is so the dough has time to settle and does not tear when you try to slice it (it's a little like slicing into a piping hot loaf of bread straight from the oven).

After the loaf has had its resting time, heat the oven to 150°C/130°C fan/300°F and line a large baking sheet with non-stick baking parchment.

Carefully peel the parchment off the loaf and, using a sharp bread knife, cut the whole loaf into slices 2–3mm/¹⁄₁₆–⅛in thick. Arrange them tightly on the baking sheet and bake in the oven for about 20 minutes, turning each *Zwieback* over halfway through so that both sides are crisped up equally.

Remove the *Zwieback* from the oven and transfer to a wire rack to cool completely. Stored in an airtight container, these will keep well for up to 2 months.

Pictured on page 119

Zwieback mit kandierten Früchten, Kirschen und Pekannüssen
Cherry, pecan and candied fruit rusks

MAKES ABOUT 30

Adding glacé cherries brings a pop of festive colour as well as an irresistible Turkish delight-like quality to a basic Zwieback recipe.

3 egg whites
60g (⅓ cup minus
   1 tsp) caster
   (superfine) sugar
1 tsp vanilla extract
125g (1 cup minus
   1 tbsp) plain
   (all-purpose) flour
Pinch of fine sea salt

40g (1½oz) mixed peel
60g (2oz) glacé
   cherries, halved
40g (1½oz) crystallized
   ginger, roughly
   chopped
50g (1¾oz) raisins
80g (3oz) pecans,
   roughly chopped

Heat the oven to 180°C/160°C fan/350°F and line a 450g (1lb) loaf tin (pan) with non-stick baking parchment that hangs substantially over the edges (this is important because the loaf will be wrapped up in this parchment before the second bake).

Put the egg whites into the bowl of a free-standing electric mixer (or in a large bowl using a hand-held electric whisk) and whisk on high speed until stiff peaks form. Reduce the speed of the whisk slightly and add the sugar, one tablespoon at a time, whisking all the while, until it's all incorporated and has turned into a glossy meringue. Now add the vanilla extract and whisk for a further couple of seconds.

Add half the flour along with the salt to the meringue mixture and fold it through gently, using a large metal spoon. Now add the remaining flour along with all the remaining ingredients and fold them in the same way, trying to knock as little air out as possible.

Gently spoon the mixture into the prepared loaf tin, levelling the top as best you can with the back of the spoon.

Bake in the oven for 25–30 minutes until firm to the touch and only just starting to turn golden brown. Lift it out gently onto a wire rack with the parchment still attached. Allow to cool completely before wrapping the parchment around it so that it's sealed. Leave to sit for 5 hours (or overnight) – this is so the dough has some time to settle and does not tear when you try to slice it (it's a little like slicing into a piping hot loaf of bread straight from the oven).

After the loaf has had its resting time, heat the oven to 150°C/130°C fan/300°F and line a large baking sheet with non-stick baking parchment.

Carefully peel the parchment off the loaf and, using a sharp bread knife, cut the whole loaf into slices 2–3mm/¹⁄₁₆–⅛in thick. Arrange them tightly on the baking sheet and bake in the oven for 20 minutes, turning each *Zwieback* over halfway through so that both sides are crisped up equally.

Remove the *Zwieback* from the oven and transfer to a wire rack to cool completely. Stored in an airtight container, these will keep well for up to a month.

Also pictured: Biberle *(p.73),* Springerle *(p.120),* Schokoküsschen *(p.153)*

Schokoladen-Ingwer-Biscotti
Chocolate and ginger biscotti

MAKES ABOUT 30

Double bake aside, these are the most simple biscuits you could ever make. All the ingredients just get mixed together with a wooden spoon in one large bowl before they are baked.

200g (1½ cups) plain (all-purpose) flour
1 tsp baking powder
Pinch of fine sea salt
100g (½ cup) soft light brown sugar
3 eggs

50g (1¾oz) dark chocolate, roughly chopped
50g (1¾oz) almonds, chopped
75g (2½oz) candied ginger, chopped
1–2 tbsp demerara sugar, for sprinkling

Heat the oven to 180°C/160°C fan/350°F and line a large baking sheet with non-stick baking parchment.

Put all of the ingredients into a large bowl and stir them together with a wooden spoon until a dense, damp dough forms.

Spoon the dough onto the lined sheet and shape into a log about 25cm/10in long and around 8–10cm/3¼–4in in diameter. The dough is pretty tacky and so won't look all that neat, but will even out in the oven. Sprinkle demerara over the top.

Bake for 25–30 minutes until firm to the touch and just golden – it should be cooked through but not hard, more like a firm sponge in texture with a crisper outer edge.

Transfer onto a wire rack to cool completely – this is important as the chocolate also needs to be cool before you cut the biscuits or they will end up being a streaky mess.

Set the lined baking sheet aside, ready for the second bake, and reduce the oven temperature to 150°C/130°C fan/300°F.

On a chopping board, and using a sharp serrated bread knife, cut the log into slices 7.5mm/⅓in thick. Arrange tightly on the lined baking sheet and bake for 25 minutes, turning them all over halfway through, until crisp on both sides.

Take out of the oven and transfer to a wire rack to cool completely. Stored in an airtight container, these will keep for a month or more.

Schokoladen-Biscotti
Double chocolate biscotti

MAKES ABOUT 30

These biscuits could quite easily be triple chocolate by simply upping the quantity and kind of chocolate to the mix as well. If that sounds like your thing, try adding 50g (1¾oz) white or milk chocolate to this recipe to make them even more indulgent. I like to get the extra chocolate hit instead by eating them alongside or dipped into a hot cocoa (see page 245 for hot chocolate with – or without – rum).

170g (1¼ cups) plain (all-purpose) flour
20g (¾oz) unsweetened cocoa powder
1 tsp baking powder
Pinch of fine sea salt
150g (¾ cup) dark brown sugar
3 eggs
1 tsp vanilla extract
80g (3oz) dark chocolate, roughly chopped
50g (1¾oz) almonds or hazelnuts, roughly chopped
1–2 tbsp demerara sugar, for sprinkling

Heat the oven to 180°C/160°C fan/350°F and line a large baking sheet with non-stick baking parchment.

Put all of the ingredients except the demerara into a large mixing bowl and stir them together with a wooden spoon until a dense, damp dough forms.

Spoon the dough onto the lined sheet and shape into a log about 25cm/10in long and around 8–10cm/3¼–4in in diameter. The dough is pretty tacky and so won't look all that neat, but will even out in the oven. Sprinkle demerara over the top.

Bake for 25–30 minutes until firm to the touch and just golden – it should be cooked through but not hard, more like a firm sponge in texture with a crisper outer edge.

Transfer onto a wire rack to cool completely – this is important as the chocolate also needs to be cool before you cut the biscuits otherwise they will end up being a streaky mess.

Set the lined baking sheet aside, ready for the second bake, and reduce the oven temperature to 150°C/130°C fan/300°F.

On a chopping board, cut the log into slices 7.5mm/⅓in thick, using a sharp serrated bread knife. Arrange the biscuits tightly on the lined baking sheet and bake for a further 25 minutes, turning them all over halfway through, until crisp on both sides.

Take out of the oven and transfer to a wire rack to cool completely. Stored in an airtight container, these will keep for a month or more.

Süße Früchtebrote

SWEET FRUIT BREADS

Rich, dense and chewy loaves made with dried fruit and spices are an important and longstanding part of Advent baking in Bavaria, Austria and many Alpine regions. High in natural fruit sugar and packed full of goodness, they're akin to an energy bar and make a brilliant snack while out on the mountains or ski slopes.

My favourite type of fruit bread is made with pears, called *Kletze* or *Hutze* when dried, which grow in abundance in this corner of Europe. Generally speaking, unless you make it yourself, you'll only find *Kletzenbrot* in small regional Alpine villages today. But the love of sticky, sweet fruit breads has spanned far and wide and a more general *Früchtebrot* (fruit bread) is available all over Germany during the Advent period.

Some of the more traditional fruit bread recipes I have come across take a couple of days to make. Not just because the fruit needs to be soaked for a period of time, but also because they are leavened with sourdough, which needs to be 'fed' and looked after before a slow double rise. I'm not averse to things in the kitchen taking time, particularly where baking is concerned, but in all honesty the best versions of *Früchtebrot* to come out of our home oven are actually the quickest loaves, using just baking powder or no raising agents at all.

Früchtebrot
Rich fruit loaf

MAKES 1 SMALL LOAF

This fruit bread is very similar to the sort of rich fruit cakes we eat in Britain at Christmas time, and although you can eat it straight away, it gets better with time, so it's worth baking it a couple of weeks before Advent or Christmas. While I tested this recipe separately with yeast, sourdough and baking powder, interestingly the best results came about when I baked it with no leavener at all.

Rye flour is lower in gluten than most wheat flours and so it doesn't rise as much anyway. In this spiced orange scented fruit cake, the rye creates a dense, nutty crumb which becomes softer the longer you keep it for, so it needs to be stored for at least a week (ideally 2–3 weeks) before eating.

75g (2½oz) dried figs, finely chopped
75g (2½oz) prunes, finely chopped
75g (2½oz) dried apricots, finely chopped
75g (2½oz) currants
75g (2½oz) mixed peel
1 tbsp brandy (or water, or orange juice)
100g (3½oz) unsalted butter, at room temp

75g (⅓ cup plus 2 tsp) soft light brown sugar
75g (⅔ cup) rye flour
Pinch of fine sea salt
1 tsp ground cinnamon
½ tsp ground cloves
¼ tsp grated nutmeg
2 eggs
Finely grated zest of 1 orange
75g (2½oz) hazelnuts, roughly chopped

ut the figs, prunes, dried apricots, currants and mixed peel into a bowl, spoon over the brandy and set aside for 1 hour.

Heat the oven to 140°C/120°C fan/280°F and line a 450g (1lb) loaf tin (pan) with non-stick baking parchment.

While the oven is heating, cream the butter and sugar together in a mixing bowl until pale and fluffy. Add the flour, salt, spices, egg and orange zest and beat together with a wooden spoon. Now add the boozy dried fruit (and any liquid) and chopped hazelnuts and stir through. Spoon the mixture into the prepared tin, smoothing the top with the back of a spoon. Bake for 2 hours until golden.

Turn out gently onto a wire rack to cool completely. Once cool, wrap tightly in a double layer of foil and store in an airtight container for at least a week before eating. This will keep well for 2 months and beyond.

Kletzenbrot
Dried pear fruit loaf

I first ate a slice of Kletzenbrot *one evening while sitting in front of a roaring fire in a small town called Ehrwald on the border between Bavaria and Austria. I went to bed and quite literally dreamed of the rich, chewy, treacly loaf. It snowed that night on the high peaks that were visible from our guesthouse window, and as I sat drinking coffee and eating more* Kletzenbrot *for breakfast, it felt as though I still hadn't woken from my Alpine dream.*

The dried pears (Kletzen) traditionally used in this recipe are shrivelled and dark in colour, looking more like some form of dried seaweed or mushroom than a sweet fruit. It's hard to get hold of them over here in the UK and so instead I use regular dried pears, treated with sulphur to keep their yellow colour.

The fruit for this loaf is usually soaked in water overnight so that it plumps up and rehydrates, but I like to use tea instead to make up for the loss of darkness and deep flavour that Kletzen would bring. This is one of my favourite things to eat with cheese and is almost as important as the cheese itself on our Christmas Eve cheese board each year.

250g (9oz) dried pears, roughly chopped
75g (2½oz) dried figs, roughly chopped
100g (3½oz) prunes, roughly chopped
75g (2½oz) raisins
275ml (1 cup plus 1 tbsp) hot strong black tea
100g (3½oz) walnut pieces

75g (⅔ cup) rye flour
75g (½ cup) plain (all-purpose) flour
1 tsp baking powder
Pinch of fine sea salt
1 tsp ground cinnamon
½ tsp ground cloves
¼ tsp grated nutmeg
60g (⅓ cup minus 1 tsp) dark brown sugar

Put the dried pears, figs, prunes and raisins into a mixing bowl. Pour over the black tea and mix together. Put a tea towel over the bowl and set aside overnight to soak.

The next day, heat the oven to 150°C/130°C fan/300°F and line a large baking sheet with non-stick baking parchment.

Add the rest of the ingredients to the soaked fruit and stir with a wooden spoon until a sticky, fruit-studded batter is formed – if it gets too hard to stir, use your hands to mix it.

Spoon the batter into a log shape (about 4cm/1½in tall, 35cm/14in long and 10cm/4in wide) onto the prepared baking sheet. It isn't easy to shape and so won't be perfect, but the rustic look adds to its charm.

Bake for 1½ hours until brown all over, checking it after an hour: if you feel it's getting too brown, cover with a piece of foil for the remainder of the baking time.

Cool on a wire rack and, once fully cool, wrap tightly with a double layer of foil. Store in an airtight tin and this will keep well for 6 weeks. Like most rich fruit cakes this loaf becomes softer the longer you keep it for, so needs to be stored for at least a week (ideally 2–3 weeks) before eating. Slice thinly to serve.

Christbrot
Christmas bread with dried fruit

MAKES 1 LOAF (SERVES ABOUT 6)

Christbrot is very similar to a Weihnachtsstollen, but lighter in texture, and is best eaten freshly baked without needing time to mature. This is one of the reasons why a Christbrot is more popular to bake at home than a Stollen each year. It isn't hard to make Christbrot but the method involves a triple rise, so you'll need to set a morning or afternoon aside if you choose to make it.

75g (2½oz) mixed peel
50g (1¾oz) raisins
50g (1¾oz) currants
1 tbsp dark rum
300g (2¼ cups) plain (all-purpose) flour, plus extra for dusting
40g (3½ tbsp) caster (superfine) sugar
½ tsp fine sea salt
Finely grated zest of ½ lemon
Finely grated zest of ½ orange
50g (3½ tbsp) unsalted butter, softened

1 egg
18g (⅔oz) fresh yeast, or 9g (⅓oz) dried
70ml (⅓ cup minus 2 tsp) tepid whole milk
50g (1¾oz) flaked (slivered) almonds

TO COAT
50g (3½ tbsp) unsalted butter, melted
40g (3½ tbsp) vanilla sugar (see page 12)
40g (4½ tbsp) icing (confectioners') sugar

ut the mixed peel, raisins and currants into a bowl, pour over the rum and set aside to infuse while you prepare the dough.

Put the flour, sugar, salt and citrus zests into a large bowl and mix together with a wooden spoon, then add the soft butter and egg. Crumble the yeast (or sprinkle if using dried) into the tepid milk and stir to dissolve. Pour the yeasted milk into the flour mixture and, using your hands, bring the ingredients together into a rough dough. Tip the dough onto a floured surface and knead for about 10 minutes until it becomes more elastic. Form it into a ball and nestle it into the bottom of the bowl. Cover the bowl with a tea towel and set aside in a warm spot to rise for 1–3 hours until almost doubled

in size. (Alternatively put the flour, sugar, salt and citrus zests into the bowl of a free-standing electric mixer fitted with a dough hook. Add the butter and egg. Pour in the yeasted milk and knead for 5 minutes until the dough is elastic. Cover the bowl and set aside, as above.)

Knock the dough back with your fist and add the almonds and boozy dried fruit (along with any liquid). Knead the fruit and nuts through for a few minutes until evenly incorporated. Form the dough into a ball and return it to the bowl. Cover with the tea towel and set aside in a warm spot for about 20 minutes for a short second rise.

Form the dough into a round loaf shape and place it on a baking sheet lined with non-stick baking parchment. Cover with a tea towel and leave somewhere warm to rise for a final 30 minutes. Heat the oven to 190°C/170°C fan/375°F.

Bake in the oven for 35–40 minutes until brown all over and cooked through, checking after 25 minutes; if it is getting too brown cover it with a piece of foil for the remainder of the baking time.

Transfer to a wire rack and brush with the melted butter repeatedly until all the butter is used up. Sprinkle with the vanilla sugar, then sift over the icing sugar.

This is best eaten within a couple of hours after it's baked. Or you can wrap it in foil and store in an airtight tin; it will keep for up to 3 days, after which it is still fine to toast for a further 2 days.

Marzipanplätzchen

MARZIPAN BISCUITS

I can't imagine a Christmas (or Easter) where marzipan baked goods don't feature. From the big hitters like marzipan-filled *Stollen* and rich marzipan-studded fruit cakes such as *Gugelhupf*, to small chewy biscuits that you can pop into your mouth in one – marzipan really is at the heart of winter festivities.

In this chapter I've written recipes for two of my favourite festive marzipan treats – *Biberle* and *Bethmännchen*. While both are classed as 'biscuits' I feel they straddle between a baked good and a confection, making them a truly versatile addition to a *Bunter Teller*.

Dominosteine are also a classic, much-loved bite-sized marzipan biscuit, made up of layered marzipan, gingerbread and jelly enrobed in chocolate. I haven't written a recipe for them here, but there's no doubt that they deserve a mention under this chapter. Truth be told, they're fiddly and I rarely make them at home, opting instead for the ease and precision of store-bought versions. While I take pride in a *Bunter Teller* featuring homemade biscuits, I'm not averse to the odd store-bought confection either – life's too short!

Biberle
Spiced marzipan bites

MAKES ABOUT 50

Biberle are little bite-sized prisms of golden marzipan wrapped up in a blanket of soft honey-sweetened gingerbread dough. They're slightly crunchy when first baked but soften over time, especially if you add a slice of apple to the tin, and I actually like them best after a week or two.

I tried to make a filling using commercial marzipan mixed with ground almonds but didn't have any success. I'm sorry to say these can only be made well with homemade marzipan (see page 230) or Marzipanrohmasse (almond paste). It's worth the effort of making the marzipan for these special biscuits, though, or hunting down some almond paste online.

125g (⅓ cup) honey
50g (¼ cup) soft light brown sugar
40g (3 tbsp) unsalted butter
200g (1½ cups) plain (all-purpose) flour, plus extra for dusting
Pinch of fine sea salt
1 tsp baking powder

2 tsp *Lebkuchengewürz* spice mix (see page 26) or 1 tsp ground cinnamon mixed with ½ tsp ground ginger, ¼ tsp ground cloves and ¼ tsp ground cardamom
280g (10oz) homemade marzipan (see page 230, or almond paste, see introduction)

Heat the oven to 180°C/160°C fan/350°F and line two baking sheets with non-stick baking parchment.

Melt the honey, sugar and butter in a saucepan over a medium heat, stirring with a wooden spoon until the sugar has dissolved and the mixture is nicely viscous (the idea is not to cook this but rather to combine it evenly).

Put the flour, salt, baking powder and spices into a mixing bowl and stir to combine. Pour in the honey mixture and mix with a wooden spoon until a stiff dough is formed; use your hands if it's too hard with a spoon. Divide the dough into four equal parts.

Divide the marzipan into four equal pieces and roll each one out into a 20cm/8in long sausage.

Roll out one piece of the dough on a lightly floured surface to a rectangle 20cm/8in long and around 10cm/4in wide. Place a marzipan sausage on a long edge closest to you and roll it up away from you, bringing the dough around it. Roll this back and forth gently on the work surface so that the join isn't visible anymore.

Slice the sausage at an angle to create little triangle shapes, where the base of each is around 1.5cm/½in and the point is 5mm/⅛in. Lay the *Biberle* on a prepared baking sheet with 1cm/⅜in space in between each one, to allow for spreading. Repeat this process with the remaining dough and marzipan.

Bake in the oven for about 10 minutes until firm and just turning golden – they will firm up slightly on cooling. Transfer to a wire rack to cool completely.

Stored in an airtight tin, these will keep well for a month or more.

Baked biscuits pictured on pages 30–31

Bethmännchen
Almond domes

These little sweet treats from the city of Frankfurt have something of the exotic about them. The orange blossom water gives them a Turkish delight quality, which fits in very well with Christmas time.

The chewy marzipan domes are adorned with 3 blanched almonds pressed into their sides and I've always thought they look rather like little crowns, especially because they're brushed with egg yolk before being baked, which gives them a golden sheen.

210g (1¾ cups) ground almonds (almond flour)

15g (2 tbsp) cornflour (cornstarch)

100g (¾ cup minus ½ tbsp) icing (confectioners') sugar

Pinch of fine sea salt

50g (1¾oz) marzipan, grated

1 tsp almond extract

1 tsp orange blossom water

1 egg white, whisked to stiff peaks

120g (4oz) blanched almonds

1 egg yolk, loosened with a fork

eat the oven to 180°C/160°C fan/350°F and line a baking sheet with non-stick baking parchment.

Mix the ground almonds, cornflour, icing sugar, salt and grated marzipan together in a bowl. Add the almond extract and orange blossom water and stir through. Now mix in the egg white and bring it all together with your hands into a ball of dense dough.

Pinch off cherry-tomato-sized pieces of dough and roll each into a ball between the palms of your hands. Place on the baking sheet and press 3 blanched almonds vertically (pointy side facing up) into the sides of the dough as though they were forming the corners of a triangle. Brush each one with egg yolk.

Bake in the oven for 10–12 minutes until just golden all over but still soft in the centre. Transfer onto a wire rack to cool. Stored in an airtight tin, these will keep well for a month.

Also pictured: Zimtsterne (p.114), Springerle (p.120), Doppeldecker (p.156), Rumkugeln (p.223)

7

Weihnachtsmärkte

CHRISTMAS MARKETS

German Christmas markets are quite something to behold. The little pop-up wooden huts form villages within cities as they fill up squares and wind down cobbled streets. Look up and you'll see a canopy of fairy lights leading you from stall to stall. Your nose will also guide you towards wherever a market is taking place, for the air will be tinged with cinnamon and clove. Breathe in deeply and your lungs will fill with the scents of pine, spice, smoke, chestnuts roasting, wine and street food. The makeshift kitchens housed inside chalet-style cladding are engulfed in clouds of steam as *Germknödel* and *Dampfnudeln* (steamed yeasted dumplings) cook and ladles of *Glühwein* are sloshed into mugs. There is something undeniably romantic and mysterious about all of this taking place in the cold air. Everything twinkles, it feels magical, whimsical, almost like a fairy tale in which you've been cast under a Christmas spell.

We're drawn to the *Weihnachtsmarkt* each year like creatures of habit, and what we eat has become almost like ritual: to start we buy some *Reibekuchen* (fried potato cakes) — top of our list, despite regularly eating them at home.

They never taste better than eaten off a flimsy paper plate in the near freezing air next to jolly strangers. Next we head for a *Flammkuchen* stall and share a slab of thin, crisp dough topped with soured cream and onions. The boys like *Bratwurst*, I did too as a child, but these days I opt for *Feuerlachs* — salmon nailed to a plank of wood and cooked around a fire, catching a whiff of woodsmoke as it burnishes — served in a crisp bun with mustard, dill and horseradish mayonnaise. After this we're all ready for a drink, *Glühwein* for me and *Kinderpunsch* for the boys. I pay the extra *Pfand* (deposit) each year to keep our mugs, of which we have a growing collection. We choose some form of fried dough for dessert and a *Schaumkuß* each (mallow on a wafer base covered in chocolate, much like a teacake) before wandering through the stalls.

Every year as we walk among the throngs of people, also here to soak up the unique festive atmosphere, I tell myself it will be my last *Weihnachtsmarkt*. I don't need to buy another ornament or eat another sausage or drink any more overpriced pre-mixed *Glühwein*, yet each year I return, unable to break free from the spell.

Gebrannte Mandeln
Cinnamon roast almonds

One of the first smells to hit you when you walk around a Christmas market is that of warm cinnamon-roasted nuts floating in the cold air. Sold in little paper cones straight from the huge roasting pan, there's nothing quite like eating them still warm as they squeak between your teeth.

Of all the recipes I tested for this book, this was the most tricky to master. They aren't actually difficult to make once you get the hang of it, but therein lies their secret, for you need to have a watchful eye and a feel for the caramelizing sugar – it's a recipe that requires your attention and attendance at the stovetop from start to finish. This is no hardship, though – standing over this pan of roasting nuts time and time again, breathing in the cinnamon steam, until I finally mastered the recipe, has been one of the highlights of writing this book. And if you fail, as I did many a time in the initial testing process, you will end up with an almond brittle instead, which is by no means a bad thing either.

150g (¾ cup) granulated sugar
75ml (5 tbsp) water
2 tsp ground cinnamon
1 tsp vanilla extract
¼ tsp fine sea salt
200g (7oz) whole almonds

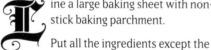Line a large baking sheet with non-stick baking parchment.

Put all the ingredients except the almonds into a large frying pan (skillet). Heat over a high heat, stirring continuously with a wooden spoon until the sugar has dissolved and the mixture starts to bubble. Now add the almonds and stir again. Turn the heat down a little so the sugar doesn't burn but continues to bubble rapidly. Stir the mixture once after 3 minutes.

At some point between 6 and 8 minutes you will notice that the sugar will start to crystallize again as the water evaporates; this is a good sign. When you notice this happening, turn the heat down a touch more and carry on cooking for a minute or two, stirring just once until most of the moisture has gone. At this point start stirring the nuts continuously to help caramelize the sugar. Once you notice the sugar start turning to caramel, take off the heat and give the nuts one last stir before tipping them out onto the prepared sheet. You're aiming for nuts that are half caramelized and half crunchy with sugar, giving them a bumpy textured finish.

Use two forks to separate the nuts on the sheet while they are still warm. Allow to cool fully on the sheet before storing in an airtight container, where they will keep well for around 2 weeks.

Weihnachtsschmalzgebäck
Christmas fried dough

MAKES ABOUT 20 (SERVES 4–6)

Schmalzgebäck (directly translated as 'lard pastry', so called because the dough was originally fried in lard and/or enriched with lard) is the blanket term for fried dough in Germany and it's not only popular during Christmas and New Year, but also at Kirchweih, a celebration organized by the Church, much like a village fête. Basically, fried dough goes hand in hand with any kind of festivities and Schmalzgebäck, rich in butter and eggs and often flavoured with wine, is the best.

Unlike doughnuts, these are not pillowy; instead they're crunchy on the outside with a soft interior. They crisp up as they cool, so it's best not to eat them directly out of the pan. I find them particularly good with a glass of Eiswein or sweet sherry, and the boys love them with hot chocolate.

A similar shortcrust-type dough is also used to make Schneebällchen, deep-fried 'snowballs', which, as their names suggests, are round in shape and often covered in white chocolate.

1 litre (4½ cups) sunflower oil
250g (1¾ cups plus 2 tbsp) plain (all-purpose) flour, plus extra for dusting
75g (⅓ cup) unsalted butter, melted
40g (3½ tbsp) caster (superfine) sugar, plus extra for sprinkling
Pinch of fine sea salt
1 tsp vanilla extract
1 egg, beaten
¾ tsp baking powder
1 tbsp white wine, sherry or mead

ine a large baking sheet with kitchen paper.

Heat the oil in a large, heavy-based saucepan over a high heat to 170°C/338°F, or until a cube of bread dropped into it starts fizzing on impact and turns golden after a few seconds. At this point turn the heat down to medium.

While the oil is coming up to temperature, put the remaining ingredients into a bowl and mix together with a wooden spoon until it becomes too stiff to mix further, at which point use your hands to bring it together. Knead for a few minutes until a supple but firm dough is formed.

Roll out the dough on a lightly floured surface to a thickness of 3–5mm/⅛in. Using a pastry cutter or a sharp knife, cut out rectangles of 10 × 4cm/4 × 1½in. Make a slit in the centre of the rectangle stopping just 1cm/⅜in shy of the short ends. Carefully lift the piece of dough up, take one of the ends and thread it through the slit, twisting it back into position from underneath. Usually this is done with both sides, but I find that too fiddly and so leave it with just one twist.

Working in batches of 4–5 at a time, gently lower the dough into the hot oil and fry for 1–3 minutes until golden all over, turning once to ensure even cooking. Lift out with a slotted spoon and drain on the lined baking sheet.

Once all the dough is fried, sprinkle generously with sugar and serve.

Quarkbällchen
Quark fritters

SERVES 4–6

Another form of fried dough popular at Christmas markets are Quarkbällchen *– little bite-sized pillows of* Quark-*enriched dough. These are surprisingly light and very easy to make, and they cook in a matter of minutes.*

I like to keep the dough sugarless so they can be either savoury or sweet, for they are just as delicious served with a sprinkling of salt and some grated cheese over the top as they are dusted with the more traditional icing sugar. Sometimes I also add a little fresh thyme to the batter for the savoury version and, for the sweet, a little cinnamon to the sugar.

1 litre (4½ cups) sunflower oil
225g (1 cup) *Quark*
2 eggs
180g (1⅓ cups) plain (all-purpose) flour
40g (¼ cup) cornflour (cornstarch)
½ tsp bicarbonate of soda (baking soda)
¾ tsp baking powder
Pinch of fine sea salt
Icing (confectioners') sugar, for dusting

Heat the oil in a large, heavy-based saucepan (skillet) over a high heat to 170°C/338°F, or until a cube of bread dropped in starts to fizz on contact and turns golden after a few seconds. Line a baking sheet with kitchen paper.

While the oil is heating, make the batter. Put all the ingredients except the icing sugar into a bowl and beat together with a wooden spoon until a stiff dough is formed.

Once the oil is hot enough, spoon small teaspoons of the dough into the oil, around 12 at a time, and fry for about 3 minutes, turning every now and then with a slotted spoon until golden brown all over. (The uncooked dough is quite sticky so you may need to wet your index finger to carefully help release the dough from the spoon and into the oil.)

Using a slotted spoon, take the fritters out of the oil and place them onto the lined sheet, to soak up any excess oil. Sprinkle generously with icing sugar and serve warm.

Flammkuchen
Flammkuchen

Flammkuchen

MAKES 2 (SERVES 2 AS A MAIN OR 4–6 AS A SNACK)

Flammkuchen, often dubbed as 'German pizza', is a very thin and crisp piece of dough topped with soured cream, onions and Schinken (cured ham). It originates from the German/French border region of Alsace – traditionally baked in a wood oven, it was invented by bakers to test the temperature of their ovens; if the oven was hot enough for bread the Flammkuchen *would only take a minute to cook.*

The dough is actually very similar to a Strudel dough, or rough filo (just flour, oil and water) and is incredibly easy to make. It's important when making this at home to heat the baking sheet up in the oven first as this ensures a crisp base, or if you have a pizza stone that's even better. I've given some suggestions for my favourite alternative flavour combinations below the recipe, but really anything goes.

FOR THE DOUGH

200g (1½ cups) plain (all-purpose) flour, plus extra for dusting
3 tbsp rapeseed oil
80ml (⅓ cup) water
Pinch of fine sea salt

150ml (⅝ cup) soured cream or crème fraîche

1 small onion, finely diced
150g (5oz) brown mushrooms, finely sliced
Flaky sea salt
Rapeseed oil, for drizzling
½ tbsp fresh thyme leaves

Heat the oven to 220°C/200°C fan/430°F. Place two large baking sheets in the oven to heat.

To make the dough, put all of the ingredients into a large bowl and mix using your hands. Knead for a couple of minutes until a supple, silky dough is formed. Divide the dough in half. On a floured surface, roll each half out as thinly as possible. So long as it fits on the baking sheet it doesn't matter what shape it is, although I aim for a rough oval.

Take the sheets out of the oven and lay the dough on top; this can be a little fiddly – I use a pizza shovel to do this but a large flat spatula or a hand supporting the underside centre of the dough while you move it also works.

Working quickly, spread the soured cream evenly across each piece of dough and scatter the onion and mushrooms over the top. Sprinkle with sea salt and drizzle with a little rapeseed oil. Bake for 15–18 minutes until the edges are crisp and the *Flammkuchen* is starting to burnish on top. Sprinkle with thyme, slice into portions and serve immediately.

VARIATIONS

Schinken – Replace the mushrooms with 200g (7oz) finely diced *Schinken* or streaky bacon.

Goat's cheese and honey – Switch the mushrooms for 200g (7oz) goat's cheese. Drizzle 1 tbsp honey on each portion, and sprinkle with thyme and some snipped chives before serving.

Pesto and tomato – Add 2 tbsp pesto to the soured cream and switch the mushrooms for 180g (6oz) cherry tomatoes (halved). Add a handful of rocket (arugula) at the end instead of the thyme.

Red pepper and black olive – Add ½ tsp sweet paprika to the soured cream. Switch the mushrooms for a finely sliced red (bell) pepper. Slice a handful of black olives in half and scatter them over both *Flammkuchen*. I like to add some fresh basil to this once it's out of the oven.

Reibekuchen
Potato cakes

A snack that is equally as popular made at home or eaten from a kiosk on the street, these little crisp potato cakes are loved up and down the country. You can always tell in which kitchens Reibekuchen are being cooked because, no matter how cold it is outside, the windows will be flung wide open.

The potatoes release quite a lot of starchy liquid when they are grated, but with the addition of flour and a couple of eggs this transforms into a batter, which is the glue that holds these little 'cakes' together.

It's custom to eat these with Apfelmus (apple sauce) and/or Rübenkraut (sugar beet syrup), but this sweet and savoury combination can seem a little odd to those who haven't grown up with it — a little like the American way of eating waffles, maple syrup and bacon together, I suppose.

1kg (2lb 3oz) potatoes, peeled and grated
1 onion, grated
4 tbsp plain (all-purpose) flour
Pinch of fine sea salt
2 eggs
Sunflower oil, for frying

Lay some kitchen paper in a dish.

Put the potatoes and onion into a large mixing bowl. Using your hands, mix them together until the onion is evenly dispersed. Sprinkle in the flour and salt and mix again so that everything is coated in the flour. Now add the eggs and mix through.

Heat a 2mm/¹⁄₁₆in depth of oil in a large frying pan (skillet) over a high heat. Once hot, spoon tablespoons of the mixture into the pan, flattening and spreading them a little with the back of the spoon. I usually fit 5 into the pan at once (1 in the middle and 4 around it). Fry on each side for 2–3 minutes until golden brown. You may need to turn the heat down a little if they are browning too quickly, and you might need to top up the oil in the pan halfway through cooking the batch.

Remove from the pan and place in the lined dish for a minute to soak up any excess oil.

Serve just as they are, or with apple sauce and/or *Rübenkraut*. They are also good with smoked salmon, goat's cheese or as part of a fried breakfast.

Stollen

STOLLEN

In Germany yeasted cakes are just as popular as those made with baking powder, and aren't just reserved for Christmas time, but eaten throughout the year – the most renowned being a traybake with plums on top called *Zwetschgenkuchen*. A yeasted dough also forms the base for a classic cake called *Bienenstich* (bee sting), in which two tiers are sandwiched together with a layer of custard and topped with caramelized almonds. Many *Apfelkuchen* (apple cakes) and *Streuselkuchen* are also traditionally made with yeasted dough.

Outside of her borders, the best known of German yeasted cakes, though, happen to be two Advent classics: the *Gugelhupf*, which takes its name from the shape of the tin it's baked in, and *Stollen*, a dense, butter-rich fruit cake (or bread depending on your sensibilities) that is often filled with marzipan.

Often thought of as a German version of an English Christmas fruit cake, *Stollen* is completely different and is actually eaten throughout the run-up to Christmas as well as on the day itself. While they both contain dried fruit and candied peel soaked in alcohol, and possibly some of the same spices, a *Stollen* is light in colour and more crumbly in texture than a moist, dark Christmas cake. *Stollen* should be eaten alongside a warm drink and, like many other classic German Advent recipes, is good dunked into said tea or coffee.

In this chapter I've covered two traditional baked *Stollen* recipes (*Weihnachtsstollen* and *Mohnstollen*), as well as more modern, and arguably easier to bake *Quark* versions. Also included is a recipe for *Stollen* biscuits, not at all traditional but something a little different for the *Bunter Teller*.

Weihnachtsstollen
Christmas Stollen

MAKES 1 LARGE *STOLLEN* (SERVES 10–12)

Stollen is a quintessential part of German Christmas, and the most renowned version originates from the East German city of Dresden, where it is called Christstollen. *It is sold in Christmas markets up and down the country, but in Dresden itself they even have a special festival (*Stollenfest*) just before the second Sunday of Advent, where a giant-sized Stollen is marched through crowds of appreciators and admirers on the streets to many oohs and aahs before it is cut up and sold off in pieces.*

Butter is one of the key ingredients that make a Stollen dough so rich, the others being eggs and boozy dried fruit. Just as important as what goes into the Stollen itself is what it is covered by, which is usually more butter and two layers of sugar. The first layer is a fine vanilla-scented caster sugar, and the second a flurry of snow-white icing sugar. This type of traditional Stollen requires a maturing period of a couple of weeks before it tastes its best. It's quite hard when first baked, but after some time in a tin wrapped up snugly in foil, it softens and develops a moister texture. I usually bake Stollen in the first week of December.

Often a Stollen is filled or flecked with marzipan too, which I like very much – if you choose to add marzipan to this recipe simply roll some out into a sausage shape and nestle it in the centre.

75g (2½oz) mixed peel
175g (6oz) raisins
1 tbsp dark rum
1 tsp vanilla extract
350g (2½ cups) strong
 white bread flour, plus
 extra for dusting
50g (¼ cup) caster
 (superfine) sugar
½ tsp fine sea salt
¼ tsp ground coriander
¼ tsp ground cloves
¼ tsp grated nutmeg
¼ tsp ground cardamom
Finely grated zest of
 1 lemon
150g (⅔ cup) unsalted
 butter, at room temp,
 cut into cubes

1 egg
20g (¾oz) fresh yeast,
 or 10g (⅓oz) dried
150ml (⅝ cup) tepid
 whole milk
60g (2oz) flaked
 (slivered) almonds

TO COAT
50g (3½ tbsp) unsalted
 butter, melted
50g (¼ cup) vanilla
 sugar (see page 12)
50g (generous ⅓ cup)
 icing (confectioners')
 sugar, plus extra to
 serve

ut the mixed peel and raisins into a bowl, spoon over the rum and vanilla extract and set aside to infuse while you prepare the dough.

Put the flour, sugar, salt, spices and lemon zest into a large mixing bowl and mix together with a wooden spoon. Add the butter and egg. Crumble the yeast (or sprinkle if using dried) into the tepid milk and stir to dissolve. Pour the yeasted milk into the flour mixture and, using your hands, bring the ingredients together until a rough dough is formed. Tip the dough onto a lightly floured work surface and knead with the heels of your hands for about 10 minutes until it becomes more elastic. Form it into a neat ball and nestle it into the bottom of the bowl. Cover the bowl with a tea towel and set aside in a warm spot to rise for 1–3 hours until visibly larger in size.

Continued overleaf

As the amount of butter in this dough is hefty, it won't double in size when it rises; you're looking for the dough to expand roughly by half its size again. (Alternatively, put the dry ingredients and lemon zest into the bowl of a free-standing electric mixer fitted with a dough hook. Add the butter and egg. Pour in the yeasted milk and knead for 5 minutes until the dough is elastic. Cover and set aside, as above.)

Knock the dough back with your fist and add the almonds and boozy dried fruit (along with any liquid) to the dough. Knead the fruit and nuts through for a couple of minutes until evenly incorporated. Form it into a neat ball and nestle it into the bottom of the bowl. Cover the bowl with a tea towel and set aside in a warm spot for about 20 minutes for a short second rise.

Lightly dust the work surface with flour, gently tip the dough out and roll into a rectangle 30 × 15cm/12 × 6in. Lay the dough on a large baking sheet lined with non-stick baking parchment, take one of the long sides and fold it three-quarters of the way back over the dough to create a classic *Stollen* shape. Lay a tea towel over the shaped *Stollen* and put in a warm place for a third rise of 30 minutes, by which time the *Stollen* should have risen slightly again. Heat the oven to 200°C/180°C fan/400°F.

Bake for about 50 minutes until browned all over, checking after 30 minutes; if it looks quite brown already, cover it with a layer of foil to stop it from burning (butter-rich yeasted doughs tend to colour quite easily).

Transfer the baked *Stollen* to a wire rack and, while still hot, brush all over with the melted butter, repeating until there is no butter left. Sprinkle the vanilla sugar over the top, then sift the icing sugar over that.

Allow the *Stollen* to cool fully before wrapping tightly in a double layer of foil. Store in an airtight container for at least a week (I think it's best to leave it 2) before slicing and serving. The *Stollen* will keep well for a good 2 months.

When ready to serve, dust with a little icing sugar again.

Mohnstollen
Poppy seed Stollen

SERVES 8

Poppy seeds have a distinctive old-world flavour about them. I associate them with the colder months of the year and they remind me of fur coats and mothballs. And likewise, whenever I see a fur coat out and about (not that often these days, I definitely don't own one) I taste poppy seeds in my mouth, or at least imagine that I do. The memory triggers strange connections when it comes to taste and it's such a personal thing – I'm sure, though, that I'm not alone in this one, as many German children of my generation will have had a similar experience of the winter coats coming out of the cupboards around the same time as Mohnstollen being present on the kitchen table.

I like to create a plaited pattern in this dough as it makes it a little more special for the festive time of year, but the dough can simply be folded over for ease and will taste exactly the same. It's important to grind the poppy seeds before they are baked so that their oils are released; don't be tempted to skip this part of the process.

400g (3 cups) strong white bread flour, plus extra for dusting
40g (3½ tbsp) caster (superfine) sugar
½ tsp fine sea salt
80g (⅓ cup plus 1 tsp) unsalted butter, at room temp
20g (¾oz) fresh yeast, or 10g (⅓oz) dried
125ml (½ cup) tepid milk
1 egg

FOR THE FILLING
150g (5oz) poppy seeds, ground (I use a coffee grinder)
120g (4oz) raisins
150ml (⅝ cup) hot milk
75g (6 tbsp) soft light brown sugar
1 egg yolk

FOR THE GLAZE
200g (1½ cups minus 1 tbsp) icing (confectioners') sugar, sifted
3 tbsp water

Put the flour, sugar and salt into a large mixing bowl and mix together with a wooden spoon. Add the butter and, using your fingertips, work it into the flour mixture until it resembles fine breadcrumbs. Crumble the yeast (or sprinkle if using dried) into the tepid milk and stir to dissolve. Pour the yeasted milk into the flour mixture along with the egg and, using your hands, bring the ingredients together until a rough dough is formed. Tip the dough onto a lightly floured work surface and knead with the heels of your hands for about 5 minutes until it becomes more elastic. Form it into a neat ball and nestle it into the bottom of the bowl. Cover the bowl with a tea towel and set aside in a warm spot to rise for about 1 hour, or until visibly larger in size. This dough won't double in size like a normal bread dough, as it is heavy on the butter, so long as it has grown by half its size, that is enough.

Continued overleaf

(Alternatively put the flour, sugar and salt into the bowl of a free-standing electric mixer fitted with a dough hook. Add the butter, yeasted milk and egg. Knead for 5 minutes until the dough is elastic. Cover and set aside, as above.)

While the dough is rising, make the filling. Put the ground poppy seeds and raisins into a medium bowl and pour over the hot milk. Mix and leave to one side for 15 minutes to cool. Once cooled, add the sugar and egg yolk and mix through.

Knock the dough back with your fist, lightly dust a sheet of non-stick baking parchment with flour and gently tip the dough onto it. Roll it out to a rectangle 40 × 30cm/16 × 12in, just shy of 5mm/⅛in thick. Spoon the poppy seed filling lengthwise into the centre, stopping 2cm/¾in short of each short side, and flatten it out until it is around 8cm/3¼in wide.

Using a pastry cutter or a sharp knife, cut diagonal lines at around a 45-degree angle and around 1.5cm/½in thick from the long sides into the dough, stopping 2cm/¾in before you reach the filling – it might help to visualize a Christmas tree here, so start with the short side of dough closest to you and cut towards the centre with the angle sloping upwards as you go.

Once you've cut the dough, it's now ready to plait. Fold both short sides in to ensure the filling doesn't leak out of the ends when it is baked. Now take the first diagonal strip furthest away from you and fold it into the centre, and repeat this alternately with each side until you come to the end, where you will need to tuck the very end bits of dough in neatly.

Slide the *Stollen* on the baking parchment onto a baking sheet, cover with a tea towel and set aside in a warm place to rise a second time, for around 20 minutes. Heat the oven to 200°C/180°C fan/400°F.

Bake in the oven for 20–25 minutes until golden brown. Allow to cool on the sheet.

Mix the icing sugar with the water, beating vigorously with a wooden spoon until a smooth, glossy glaze is formed. Spoon the glaze generously over the *Stollen* and leave it to one side for 30 minutes or so to set.

Best served the day it is made, but will keep well wrapped in foil in an airtight tin for up to a week.

Quarkstollen
Quark Stollen

SERVES 12

Christmas wouldn't be complete in Germany without a Stollen *in the house. A traditional Weihnachtsstollen, made with yeasted dough, is the classic version and is hard to beat, but like any rich, dense fruit cake, it needs a couple of weeks to mature after baking before it tastes its best.*

This recipe is cheating, I suppose, because it uses baking powder and bicarbonate of soda as the leavener, but the beauty of it lies in this very fact, for it means the method is simple. The Quark *makes the dough moist and works well to balance out the sweetness from the dried fruit and icing sugar, of which there is a lot – the whole idea being that it should look like a snowdrift.*

150g (5oz) raisins
50g (1¾oz) mixed peel
2 tbsp rum
400g (3 cups) plain
 (all-purpose) flour
75g (½ cup) cornflour
 (cornstarch)
125g (⅔ cup) caster
 (superfine) sugar
1½ tsp baking powder
½ tsp bicarbonate of
 soda (baking soda)
½ tsp fine sea salt
½ tsp ground cinnamon
¼ tsp ground cloves
¼ tsp grated nutmeg
¼ tsp ground cardamom
2 eggs

125g (½ cup plus
 1 tbsp) unsalted
 butter, at room temp,
 cut into cubes
250g (1 cup plus
 2 tbsp) Quark
1 tsp vanilla extract
50g (1¾oz) flaked
 (slivered) almonds
Finely grated zest of
 1 orange or lemon

TO COAT
50g (3½ tbsp) unsalted
 butter, melted
Icing (confectioners')
 sugar, for dusting

Put all the dry ingredients into a large mixing bowl and stir everything until evenly combined. Crack in the eggs, add the butter, *Quark* and dried fruit with the rum, as well as the vanilla extract, almonds and orange zest. Mix everything together with your hands until a very soft, sticky dough is formed. Leave to one side for 10 minutes to enable the bicarbonate of soda to work its magic.

Form the dough into a rectangle 30cm/12in long and about 10cm/4in wide and place on the prepared baking sheet. Bake in the centre of the oven for about 1 hour, until nutty brown all over, turning the sheet around once halfway through to ensure an even bake.

Using a pastry brush, coat the *Stollen* with the melted butter as soon as it comes out of the oven, and sift over some icing sugar. Cool completely on a wire rack.

To serve, dust the *Stollen* generously with more icing sugar. Serve sliced as it is, or with butter and jam. Stored wrapped in foil in an airtight container, this will keep well for up to 5 days.

Put the raisins and mixed peel into a bowl, pour over the rum and set aside to infuse while you prepare the dough. Heat the oven to 160°C/140°C fan/320°F and line a baking sheet with non-stick baking parchment.

Stollenplätzchen
Stollen biscuits

These are a bit of fun that I've enjoyed experimenting with while writing this book — butter-rich biscuits with Stollen flavours are set to become a tradition in our house from now on, as I hope they might in yours.

50g (½ cup minus 1 tbsp) ground almonds (almond flour)

150g (1 cup plus 2 tbsp) plain (all-purpose) flour, plus extra for dusting

12g (1½ tbsp) cornflour (cornstarch)

Pinch of fine sea salt

125g (½ cup plus 1 tbsp) unsalted butter, at room temp

100g (½ cup plus 1 tbsp) caster (superfine) sugar

½ tsp ground cinnamon

¼ tsp ground cloves

⅛ tsp grated nutmeg

¼ tsp ground ginger

Finely grated zest of ½ lemon

1 egg yolk

40g (1½oz) currants

30g (1oz) mixed peel

Icing (confectioners') sugar, for dusting

Heat the oven to 200°C/180°C fan/400°F. Line two large baking sheets with non-stick baking parchment.

Put the ground almonds, flour, cornflour and salt into a large mixing bowl. Add the butter and work it into the flour using your fingertips, until it resembles breadcrumbs. Add the sugar, spices and lemon zest and mix through. Now add the egg yolk along with the dried fruit and knead into a stiff dough.

Lightly dust the work surface with flour. Divide the dough in half and roll one half out to around a 3mm/⅛in thickness. Using a fluted cookie cutter (see pages 258–9), or a snowflake-shaped cutter, cut out biscuits and lay them on a baking sheet with 1cm/⅜in between each, to allow for spreading. Repeat with the remaining dough, then re-roll all the dough offcuts into more biscuits.

Bake in the oven for about 8 minutes until golden. Allow to cool on the sheets for a minute before transferring to a wire rack. Sift over a generous amount of icing sugar while still hot, then leave to cool completely.

Stored in an airtight tin, these will keep for up to 3 weeks.

Stollenkonfekt
Stollen bites

MAKES ABOUT 35–40

Stollenkonfekt is something that has become popular during my lifetime. It's basically mini bite-sized versions of the real thing. I like to make these moreish buttery confections with Quark and baking powder for ease, but these would also work with yeasted dough.

If you are new to the idea of Stollen, these might well be the best place for you to start.

100g (3½oz) raisins
30g (1oz) mixed peel
1 tbsp dark rum or brandy
300g (2¼ cups) plain (all-purpose) flour
50g (⅓ cup) cornflour (cornstarch)
75g (⅓ cup plus 1 tbsp) caster (superfine) sugar
1 tsp baking powder
½ tsp bicarbonate of soda (baking soda)
Pinch of fine sea salt
1 tsp ground cinnamon
½ tsp ground cloves
⅛ tsp grated nutmeg

Finely grated zest of 1 lemon
1 egg
120g (½ cup plus 2 tsp) unsalted butter, at room temp
200g (1 cup minus 1 tbsp) Quark
1 tsp vanilla extract

TO COAT
220g (1½ cups) icing (confectioners') sugar, sifted
130g (½ cup plus 1 tbsp) unsalted butter, melted

Heat the oven to 180°C/160°C fan/350°F. Line two large baking sheets with non-stick baking parchment.

Put the raisins and mixed peel into a bowl, pour over the rum and set aside to infuse while you make the dough.

Put the dry ingredients into a large mixing bowl and stir everything together until evenly combined. Crack in the egg, add the butter, *Quark* and dried fruit with the rum, as well as the vanilla extract. Mix everything together with your hands until a very soft, sticky dough is formed. Leave to one side for 10 minutes to enable the bicarbonate of soda to work its magic, then pinch off small, walnut-sized pieces and form them into little pillow shapes.

Place on the prepared baking sheets, leaving 2cm/¾in between each, and bake in the centre of the oven for 22–25 minutes until golden brown all over, turning the sheet around once halfway through to ensure an even bake.

While they are baking, place the sifted icing sugar in a large shallow dish.

Using a pastry brush, glaze each *Stollenkonfekt* with the melted butter as soon as they come out of the oven, then roll them around in the icing sugar (one at a time) until thickly coated. Place them on a wire rack to cool completely.

Once cool and ready to serve, dust with more icing sugar. Stored in an airtight container, these will keep well for around a week.

9

Spritzgebäck

PATTERNED BISCUITS

Spritz means squirt in German, and traditionally these biscuits (cookies) derived their shape and name from being passed through a tabletop mincer with a cookie attachment on the front, through which the dough is pushed or 'squirted' out. These days, though, you can also buy specially made cookie presses, solely for the purpose of making *Spritzgebäck*, which look a little like those sealant guns you can buy at DIY stores. Neither is expensive, and I find both very useful, but you don't need either of them to make these biscuits. A fork will work just as well at creating a pretty pattern and texture. And a freezer bag with the corner end cut off makes an admirable piping bag through which you can *spritz* your dough too.

Spritzgebäck are one of the more classic Advent biscuits and are usually made in big batches.* This is partly because there is no point making a small batch in the mincer, but mostly it is because they're loved by all, from children to grandparents, and they win the popular vote in our house. They go equally as well with a glass of warm *Kakao* (cocoa) as they do with a cup of tea or coffee, and make brilliant dunkers.

While perfectly doable on your own, *Spritzgebäck* are a great thing to make together as a family. Three pairs of hands is actually ideal: one for cranking the handle, one for pushing the dough into the mincer with a wooden spoon and one for catching the biscuits as they come out of the spout – a messy conveyor belt of festive fun. If, unlike me, you don't constantly have eager children to hand, I can imagine that making *Spritzgebäck* with a couple of friends and a glass of wine or two would be a brilliant way to spend a Sunday afternoon in December.

When freshly baked, *Spritzgebäck* are crisp and buttery. The use of granulated sugar instead of caster (superfine) in the traditional *Vanillespritzgebäck* makes them particularly crunchy. They will soften over time, though, and some people like to 'rest' *Spritzgebäck* in the tin for
a week before eating for exactly this reason.

*If the volume of biscuits per bake is too much for your needs, simply halve the recipe to make a more manageable amount.

Gewürzspritzgebäck
Christmas spiced shortbread

MAKES 80–100

I usually use the cookie press to make these because I find they look particularly festive in little wreath shapes. If you aren't so keen on icing you can sprinkle each biscuit with a little demerara sugar before baking – this adds a pleasing crunch and caramel note to the cookie.

275g (2 cups) plain (all-purpose) flour
50g (⅓ cup) cornflour (cornstarch)
50g (½ cup minus 1 tbsp) ground almonds (almond flour)
50g (½ cup minus 1 tbsp) ground hazelnuts
250g (1 cup plus 2 tbsp) unsalted butter, at room temp, cut into 2cm/¾in cubes
175g (¾ cup plus 2 tbsp) soft light brown sugar

Pinch of fine sea salt
2 tsp ground cinnamon
½ tsp ground ginger
½ tsp ground anise (or a drop of anise extract)
½ tsp ground cloves
1 tsp vanilla extract
2 tbsp milk

FOR THE GLAZE
100g (scant ¾ cup) icing (confectioners') sugar, sifted
25ml (scant 2 tbsp) just-boiled water

Heat the oven to 180°C/160°C fan/350°F and line two baking sheets with non-stick baking parchment.

Put all the ingredients into the mixing bowl of an electric mixer fitted with a paddle attachment and beat to a soft, pliable dough on a low speed for a couple of minutes. (If making by hand, put both flours, the ground almonds and ground hazelnuts into a large bowl, then work the butter in with your fingertips until it resembles breadcrumbs. Mix through the sugar, salt and spices. Add the vanilla extract and milk, and bring the dough together with your hands. Knead for 3 minutes until pliable.)

If using a cookie press, select your preferred shape, then stuff the dough into the top. Hold the press over a prepared baking sheet and click the handle to release one cookie. Repeat this process, placing each cookie 1cm/³⁄₈in apart to allow for spreading.

If using the mincer method, choose the desired attachment and place your dough in the funnel. Crank the handle with one hand, holding the other hand just below the spout to support the dough as it comes out. When the dough protrudes by 6cm/2½in, cut it off and place it on a baking sheet. Repeat this process, spacing the biscuits 1cm/³⁄₈in apart, until both sheets are full.

Bake for 8–10 minutes until just golden.

If you don't have a mincer or cookie press and are making the biscuits by hand, take small, walnut-sized pieces of dough and roll them into sausage shapes around 5cm/2in long. Place them 2cm/¾in apart on the sheets. Press a fork gently into the top edge of each biscuit and drag it down the length of the dough, flattening and lengthening it as you go. Bake as above, but allow at least 10 minutes (hand-formed biscuits tend to be thicker and so take longer to bake).

While the biscuits are baking, put the icing sugar into a bowl, pour in the just-boiled water and mix vigorously until a glossy glaze forms.

Allow the cooked biscuits to cool for a minute before transferring to a wire rack. Using a pastry brush, glaze each biscuit while still warm.

Repeat the whole process again with any remaining dough.

Store in an airtight container for up to 4 weeks.

Baked biscuits pictured on page 105

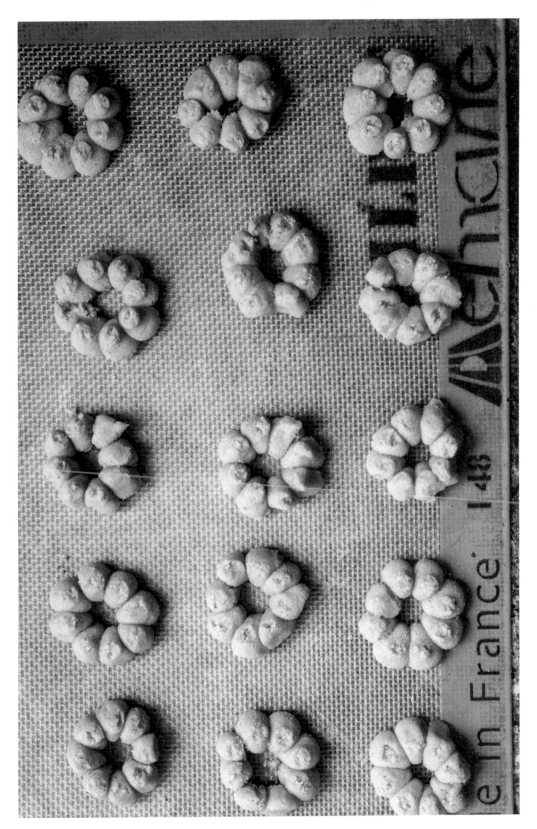

Vanillespritzgebäck
Vanilla shortbread

MAKES 80–100

More often than not I use my kitchen mixer to bring this dough together as it's much quicker and easier, especially when you're baking vast batches, but of course it's more rewarding to do it by hand if you have the time.

300g (2¼ cups) plain (all-purpose) flour
50g (⅓ cup) cornflour (cornstarch)
75g (⅔ cup) ground almonds (almond flour)
250g (1 cup plus 2 tbsp) unsalted butter, at room temp, cut into 2cm/¾in cubes

175g (¾ cup plus 2 tbsp) granulated sugar
Pinch of fine sea salt
1 tsp vanilla extract
2 tbsp milk

FOR THE CHOCOLATE-DIPPED ENDS
150g (5oz) dark chocolate, broken into pieces
¼ tsp coconut oil

Heat the oven to 180°C/160°C fan/350°F and line two baking sheets with non-stick baking parchment.

Put all the ingredients into the bowl of an electric mixer fitted with the paddle attachment and beat to a soft, pliable dough on a low speed for a couple of minutes. (If making by hand, put the flours and ground almonds into a large bowl, then work the butter in with your fingertips until it resembles breadcrumbs. Mix in the sugar and salt. Add the vanilla extract and milk and bring the dough together with your hands. Knead for 3 minutes to a pliable dough.)

If using the mincer method, choose the desired attachment and place your dough in the funnel. Crank the handle with one hand, holding the other hand just below the spout to support the dough as it comes out. When the dough protrudes by 6cm/2½in, cut it off and place it on a baking sheet. Repeat this process, spacing the biscuits 1cm/⅜in apart, until both sheets are full.

If you prefer to use a cookie press, stuff the dough into the top then hold the press over the prepared baking sheet and click the handle to release one cookie. Repeat this process, placing each cookie 1cm/⅜in apart on the sheets.

Bake for 8–10 minutes until just golden. Allow to cool on the sheet for a minute before transferring to a wire rack to cool completely.

Repeat the whole process again with any remaining dough.

If you don't have a mincer or cookie press and are making the biscuits by hand, take small, walnut-sized pieces of dough and roll them into sausage shapes around 5cm/2in long. Place them 2cm/¾in apart on the sheets. Press a fork gently into the top edge of each biscuit and drag it down the length of the dough, flattening and lengthening it as you go. Bake as above, but allow at least 10 minutes in the oven (hand-formed biscuits tend to be a little thicker and so take slightly longer to bake).

Once the biscuits are cool they are ready to brush with chocolate if you so wish. Put the chocolate and coconut oil into a heatproof bowl set over a small saucepan with a 1cm/⅜in depth of water in the bottom. Heat on low until the chocolate melts, then stir so that the coconut oil is evenly dispersed throughout. Take off the heat once the chocolate is glossy and fluid.

Using a pastry brush, paint half of each biscuit with the chocolate. Leave on the wire rack for a couple of hours to set before transferring to an airtight container for up to 4 weeks.

Also pictured: Gewürzspritzgebäck (p.102)

Schokoladen- spritzgebäck
Chocolate shortbread

MAKES 80–100

These biscuits are so deeply chocolatey that I find they need no extra embellishment with chocolate glaze or sugar coating, although you could go the extra mile if you wish.

300g (2¼ cups) plain (all-purpose) flour
50g (1¾oz) unsweetened cocoa powder
75g (⅔ cup) ground hazelnuts (or almonds)

250g (1 cup plus 2 tbsp) unsalted butter, at room temp, cut into 2cm/¾in cubes
200g (1 cup) dark brown sugar
Pinch of fine sea salt
1 tsp vanilla extract
2 tbsp milk

eat the oven to 180°C/160°C fan/350°F and line two baking sheets with non-stick baking parchment.

Put all the ingredients into the bowl of an electric mixer fitted with the paddle attachment and beat to a soft, pliable dough on a low speed for a couple of minutes. (If making by hand, put the flour, cocoa powder and ground hazelnuts into a large mixing bowl. Gently work the butter into the dry ingredients with your fingertips until it resembles fine breadcrumbs. Mix through the sugar and salt until evenly dispersed. Add the vanilla extract and milk and bring the dough together with your hands. Knead for about 3 minutes until a pliable dough is formed.)

Now follow the shaping and baking instructions for the *Vanillespritzgebäck* on page 104.

Marzipan- spritzgebäck
Marzipan shortbread

MAKES 80–100

With a weakness for all things marzipan, it's no surprise that these are my favourite Spritzgebäck.

300g (2¼ cups) plain (all-purpose) flour
125g (1 cup plus 2 tbsp) ground almonds (almond flour)
250g (1 cup plus 2 tbsp) unsalted butter, at room temp, cut into 2cm/¾in cubes

100g (3½oz) marzipan, grated
150g (¾ cup) granulated sugar
Pinch of fine sea salt
½ tsp almond extract
1–2 tbsp milk
120g (4oz) flaked (slivered) almonds

eat the oven to 180°C/160°C fan/350°F and line two baking sheets with non-stick baking parchment.

Put all the ingredients except the milk and flaked almonds into the bowl of an electric mixer fitted with a paddle attachment and beat to a soft, pliable dough, adding milk if needed. (If making by hand, put the flour and ground almonds into a large bowl then work the butter in with your fingertips until it resembles breadcrumbs. Mix through the grated marzipan, sugar and salt. Add the almond extract and bring the dough together with your hands. Knead for 3 minutes until pliable. It should be the consistency of play dough; if needed, add a little milk, one tablespoon at a time, kneading well.)

Put the flaked almonds into a shallow dish.

Now follow the shaping and baking instructions for the *Vanillespritzgebäck* on page 104, pressing each cookie into the dish of almonds before placing on the baking sheet and baking.

Weihnachtsröschen
Christmas swirls

MAKES ABOUT 40

This recipe is inspired by Austrian butter biscuits and although they aren't necessarily related to Christmas time I've taken the liberty of including a verison here, because a) they're gespritzt b) they're delicious, and c) who's to say they can't become your new Christmas favourite?

The jam, which is spooned into a thumbprint hollow, makes for a lovely festive touch.

200g (1½ cups) plain (all-purpose) flour
50g (⅓ cup) cornflour (cornstarch)
½ tsp baking powder
200g (¾ cup plus 2 tbsp) unsalted butter, at room temp, cut into 2cm/¾in cubes

80g (½ cup plus 1 tbsp) icing (confectioners') sugar
Pinch of fine sea salt
1 tsp vanilla extract
About 80g (3oz) raspberry jam (jelly)

Heat the oven to 180°C/160°C fan/350°F and line two baking sheets with non-stick baking parchment.

Put all the ingredients except the jam into the mixing bowl of an electric mixer fitted with a paddle attachment and beat to a pliable dough on a low speed for a couple of minutes. (If making by hand, put both flours and the baking powder into a large mixing bowl. Gently work the butter into the dry ingredients with your fingertips until it resembles breadcrumbs. Mix through the sugar and salt until evenly dispersed. Add the vanilla extract and bring the dough together with your hands. Knead for about 3 minutes until a pliable dough is formed.)

Slot a 1cm/⅜in star-shaped nozzle into a piping bag. Spoon the biscuit mixture into the bag, twist the top once it's all in and squeeze the dough down towards the nozzle from the twist.

Swirl circles of about 4cm/1½in in diameter onto the prepared baking sheets. The biscuits spread a bit when baked and so be sure to leave 2cm/¾in space between each one. Press a finger into the centre of each swirl to create an indent. Spoon ½ teaspoon of jam into each imprint, then transfer to the oven and bake for 10–12 minutes until light golden.

Leave on the sheets to cool for a minute before transferring to a wire rack to cool completely. They are crisp when first baked but soften soon after, and keep well for about 2 weeks in an airtight container.

NOTE

If you don't have a piping bag or find the process too much of a faff you can simply pinch off walnut-sized lumps of dough, roll them into a ball, flatten slightly, indent them in the centre with you finger and fill them with jam in the same way. They will end up being more of a rustic thumbprint-style biscuit, which is the way I used to make them when the boys were very small. I've never known a child who doesn't love to squish a pudgy finger into a bit of dough (especially sweet dough).

Gewürzplätzchen

SPICED BISCUITS

The use of spices in Christmas baking is not something unique to Germany. Spices are used the world over at this time of year and are what connect so many of our rituals and celebrations.

If you've never studded an orange with cloves before, try it. As you prick each wooden ended fragrant clove into the orange, simultaneously releasing and 'spritzing' out its citrus essential oil, your nostrils will be hit with Christmas — it doesn't matter where you are from or whether or not you've ever done this before, but something about it will ring Christmas bells in your head. Rubbing a cinnamon stick between your fingers has this same effect, as does the

heady hit of many other spices wafting from the oven, especially when used in conjunction with each other.

All of the biscuits (cookies) in this chapter are classic German Advent biscuits, though many variations along the same theme are also made in Scandinavian countries and the Netherlands too, just under different names. Some of the biscuits use one single spice only, which is usually given away by its name, *Zimtsterne* (cinnamon stars) for example, while others are flavoured by a delicate balance and mixture of spices. Advent is what binds them all together, as usually they aren't baked at any other time of year.

Spekulatius
Spiced almond biscuits

MAKES ABOUT 30

These biscuits are traditional Advent sweet treats in both the Netherlands, where they are usually eaten around the 6th December (St Nikolaus day), and in Germany, where they are eaten throughout the whole run-up to Christmas. Usually they're decorated with images relating to Nikolaus, and more often than not have windmills depicted on them.

You can also buy special wooden rolling pins with pictured squares carved into them specifically for rolling this dough out at home. I don't have one of these and I certainly don't have the patience to create the intricate decoration it would involve without using one. Instead I use pretty cutters (I think snowflakes work best) to cut out festive shapes (see pages 258–9).

Usually almond Spekulatius have a flaked almond base, but I've switched things up and adorned mine with them on top instead. These snappy (by this I mean crunchy and good to snap) biscuits are best eaten alongside a black coffee and are also brilliant crushed into a powder and mixed with melted butter to create a Christmas cheesecake or chocolate torte base.

150g (1 cup plus 2 tbsp) plain (all-purpose) flour, plus extra for dusting
50g (½ cup minus 1 tbsp) rye flour
½ tsp bicarbonate of soda (baking soda)
1½ tsp ground cinnamon
¼ tsp ground cloves
¼ tsp grated nutmeg

120g (⅔ cup) caster (superfine) sugar
Pinch of fine sea salt
125g (½ cup plus 1 tbsp) unsalted butter, at room temp
1 egg

TO FINISH
Milk, for brushing
50g (1¾oz) flaked (slivered) almonds

Put all the dry ingredients into a large mixing bowl and stir with a wooden spoon. Add the butter and mix it into the flour using your fingertips until it has the consistency of fine breadcrumbs. Add the egg and bring everything together into a dough with your hands. (Alternatively, simply put all the ingredients into the bowl of an electric free-standing mixer fitted with a paddle attachment and mix until an even dough is formed.)

Heat the oven to 190°C/170°C fan/375°F and line two large baking sheets with non-stick baking parchment.

Roll out the dough on a lightly floured surface to a 3mm/⅛in thickness. Cut out shapes with your cookie cutter (see pages 258–9) and gently transfer them onto the prepared baking sheets, leaving 1cm/⅜in between each to allow for spreading. Re-roll the dough offcuts into more biscuits. Brush the tops with milk then sprinkle some flaked almonds onto each one, pressing them down gently to ensure they stick.

Bake in the oven for 10–12 minutes until golden all over. Allow to cool on the sheets for a minute before transferring to a wire rack to cool completely.

Store in an airtight container, where they will keep well for up to 4 weeks.

Zimtsterne
Cinnamon stars

MAKES ABOUT 30

For me, and I believe many Germans would agree, Zimtsterne
belong to the classic trio of biscuits that best sum up
Adventsgebäck – Lebkuchen *and* Vanillekipferl *being the other two.*

Christmas just wouldn't be Christmas without Zimtsterne *and
they are baked at least once a week without fail in our house
throughout the month of December. If the boys had it their way
we would, in an ideal world, bake them every day.*

2 egg whites
180g (1¼ cups) icing
  (confectioners') sugar,
  plus extra for dusting
4 tsp ground cinnamon
300g (1⅔ cups)
  ground almonds
  (almond flour)

FOR THE ICING
1 egg white
100g (scant ¾ cup)
  icing (confectioners')
  sugar, sifted

Heat the oven to 180°C/160°C fan/350°F and line two baking sheets with non-stick baking parchment.

Whisk the egg whites to stiff peaks using a hand-held electric whisk or in the bowl of a free-standing electric mixer fitted with the whisk attachment. Add the icing sugar one tablespoon at a time, whisking all the while. Add the cinnamon and give it a final few seconds of whisking before folding in the ground almonds with a spatula, bringing all the ingredients together into a sticky dough.

Dust the work surface with icing sugar and roll the dough out to a 5mm/⅛in thickness. Cut star shapes out of the dough with your cookie cutter (see pages 258–9) and gently transfer them over to the baking sheet with 1cm/⅜in between each to allow for a little spreading. Re-roll all the dough offcuts into more biscuits.

Bake in the oven for 10–12 minutes until just golden on top and firm to the touch – they should still be soft inside. Allow to cool on the sheet for 5 minutes before transferring to a wire rack to cool completely.

To make the icing, whisk the egg white to stiff peaks using a hand-held electric whisk or an old-fashioned double whisk with a cranking handle (my preferred choice; one egg white is too small an amount to whisk in a free-standing kitchen machine). Fold the icing sugar into the stiff egg white until a thick, glossy icing is formed.

Spoon small amounts of icing onto each cooled biscuit and, using the tip of a knife, drag the icing out to the pointed ends of the star, ensuring the entire top of the cookie is covered. Leave out to air dry for 8 hours (overnight is ideal).

Stored in an airtight container, these will keep well for a month or more.

Weiße Pfeffernüsse
White pepper spiced biscuits

MAKES 50

Pfeffernüsse are a particular type of domed spiced biscuit that have a unique flavour owing to the use of white pepper, of which just a small amount is added, often described in older recipes as a knife tip's worth. The curious nasal sensation and warm feeling of pepper on your tongue only hits you after you have eaten your first bite, which works a kind of magic on you, enticing you to swiftly take one more bite, and in turn try 'just one more biscuit'.

Pfeffernüsse owe their domed shape and spongy texture to Hirschhornsalz (bakers' ammonia or ammonium carbonate), a traditional raising agent used throughout Germany and Scandinavia for Christmas cookies (see page 13). The ammonia which is released while Hirschhornsalz is heated in the oven smells interesting, but the gases soon vanish once the biscuits are out of the oven and leave no aftertaste.

200g (1 ½ cups) plain (all-purpose) flour
180g (1 cup) caster (superfine) sugar
1 ½ tsp ground cinnamon
¼ tsp ground cloves
¼ tsp ground white pepper
Pinch of fine sea salt
¾ tsp *Hirschhornsalz* (see introduction)

1 tbsp dark rum
2 eggs

FOR THE ICING
80g (generous ½ cup) icing (confectioners') sugar, sifted
1 tbsp water
2 tsp lemon juice

Heat the oven to 190°C/170°C fan/375°F and line two large baking sheets with non-stick baking parchment.

Put the flour, sugar, spices and salt into a mixing bowl and stir with a wooden spoon until evenly combined.

In a small glass, mix the *Hirschhornsalz* with the rum, stirring until it has dissolved. Add this to the flour mixture, followed by the eggs. Stir together with a wooden spoon until a sticky dough forms.

Flour your hands and pinch off small, teaspoon-sized pieces of dough, roll into little balls and place 3cm/1¼in apart on the lined sheets. Bake in the oven for 8–10 minutes until domed and firm but not browned.

While the biscuits are baking, make the icing by mixing the icing sugar, water and lemon juice together in a bowl until a smooth paste forms.

Allow the biscuits to cool on the sheets for 2 minutes before transferring to a wire rack. Ice while still warm by brushing the glaze on the domed tops with a pastry brush. Allow to cool completely – I tend to leave mine on the wire rack for an hour, just to ensure the icing has also set hard. Stored in an airtight container, these keep well for 4 weeks or more.

Braune Pfeffernüsse
Brown pepper spiced biscuits

MAKES 50

It's hard to know what to call these in English because 'brown pepper spiced biscuits' seems somewhat misleading as the pepper used is white, yet the biscuits are brown in colour due to the dark brown sugar and cocoa.

These are the sister biscuits to white Pfeffernüsse, *and are my preferred choice. The cocoa doesn't so much flavour as colour the dough, and the brown sugar gives them a slightly chewy toffee edge.* Braune Pfeffernüsse *are often coated in chocolate, as here, but I also like a thin lemon-scented sugar glaze that shatters between your teeth as you bite down into it, as on page 117; choose whichever coating you prefer.*

200g (1½ cups) plain (all-purpose) flour
180g (1 cup) dark brown sugar
2 tsp unsweetened cocoa powder
1½ tsp ground cinnamon
¼ tsp ground cloves
¼ tsp ground white pepper
Pinch of fine sea salt

¾ tsp *Hirschhornsalz* (see introduction)
1 tbsp dark rum
2 eggs

FOR THE CHOCOLATE GLAZE
100g (3½oz) dark chocolate, broken into pieces
¼ tsp coconut oil

Heat the oven to 190°C/170°C fan/375°F and line two large baking sheets with non-stick baking parchment.

Put the flour, sugar, cocoa powder, spices and salt into a mixing bowl and stir with a wooden spoon until evenly combined.

In a small glass, mix the *Hirschhornsalz* with the rum, stirring until it has dissolved. Add this to the flour mixture, followed by the eggs. Stir together with a wooden spoon until a sticky dough forms.

Flour your hands and pinch off small, teaspoon-sized pieces of dough, roll into little balls and place 3cm/1¼in apart on the lined sheets. Bake in the oven for 8–10 minutes until domed and firm but not browned.

Allow the biscuits to cool on the sheets for 2 minutes before transferring to a wire rack.

You can now ice while still warm by brushing sugar glaze on the domed tops with a pastry brush, as on page 117.

Alternatively, make the chocolate glaze. Put the chocolate and coconut oil into a heatproof bowl, place the bowl over a small saucepan with a 1cm/⅜in depth of water in the bottom. Turn the heat on low and wait for the chocolate to melt. Once it starts melting, stir so that the coconut oil is evenly dispersed throughout. Brush onto the domed tops of the cooled biscuits, using a pastry brush, and leave to set for an hour or so.

Stored in an airtight container, these keep well for 4 weeks or more.

Pictured on top shelf, from left to right: Walnusszwieback *(p.55),* Lebkuchenherzen *(p.29),* Braune Pfeffernüsse *with sugar glaze,* Spekulatius *without almond topping (p.113)*

Springerle
Aniseed biscuits

These biscuits, like Lebkuchen, seem to be as old as the hills. Unlike Lebkuchen, though, they aren't a biscuit I grew up baking and eating religiously over the Advent period and are something I have only learned to make recently. For many, though, Springerle — aniseed-flavoured biscuits from Swabia in Southwestern Germany — represent exactly what Advent baking is about, which is to pass on family traditions and rituals by coming together of an evening around the kitchen table to make and bake biscuits that bring us that little bit closer to our history and the generations before us, as well as creating new memories too.

Springerle are elaborately decorated using specifically carved wooden moulds, many of them family heirlooms passed down. Despite not having any family history or stories surrounding these biscuits myself, there is something about the process of making Springerle that does feel ancient and special. Having tested several variations of these biscuits I now get the hype that surrounds them, and it's quite possible that 2020 will mark the year the Springerle tradition started in our house.

Springerle are made of a simple butterless, egg-heavy dough, which involves a long period of high-speed whisking — quite how these were made in the olden days before electrical kitchen machines were around I have no idea. They are leavened with Hirschhornsalz (see page 13), which makes the biscuits 'jump up' when baked, hence their name (springen means 'to jump') — this 'jumping' process creates visible little 'feet' at the bottom of the biscuits from which the top springs. Hirschhornsalz is vital in the making of Springerle because it keeps the embossing on the biscuit sharp, a detail which would be lost through the use of baking powder.

I don't own any Springerle moulds, but I do have a drawer full of mooncake moulds from China and I think they work a treat, particularly because the Chinese folk art images of lucky fish, birds and acorns don't seem amiss amidst the flowers, horses and hearts depicted in traditional Springerle moulds. I can imagine, too, that maamoul cookie moulds would also work here. If you don't have any moulds at all, don't worry, you can simply cut out festive shapes — they certainly won't be as pretty, but close your eyes on biting into one and the taste will be the same.

Once embossed, the biscuits are laid out onto aniseed-sprinkled baking sheets and left to air dry for between 12 and 24 hours; this is so that the design has a chance to dry out and keep its shape better when baked.

The biscuits are at their best after a couple of days left in the tin, which allows the anise to penetrate through and for the dough to settle into its ideal texture. They should be crunchy on the outside with a dry, slightly chewy centre.

It's very hard to say how many biscuits this recipe yields as it all depends on the size of your moulds/cutters, so I'm going for a ballpark figure of 25–50. The recipe is easily halved should you choose not to bake so many.

4 eggs
250g (1⅓ cups) caster
(superfine) sugar
250g (1¾ cups) icing
(confectioners') sugar
Pinch of fine sea salt
500g (3¾ cups) plain
(all-purpose) flour,
plus extra for dusting

Finely grated zest
of 1 lemon
1 tsp vanilla extract
⅓ tsp *Hirschhornsalz*
(see page 13)
1 tsp water
Aniseeds, for sprinkling

ut the eggs and both sugars into the bowl of a free-standing electric mixer fitted with a whisk attachment. Whisk on high for 8–10 minutes until pale and fluffy.

Add the salt, flour, lemon zest and vanilla extract to the bowl. Dissolve the *Hirschhornsalz* in the water and add this to the rest of the ingredients. Fold everything together using a large metal spoon, until a stiff dough is formed. Set aside to rest for 1 hour.

Line a couple of sheets with non-stick baking parchment (usually I need 3 large sheets for this amount of dough) and sprinkle each sheet with a scattering of aniseeds.

Once the dough has rested, get all of your moulds ready and lightly dust the work surface (or table if you are doing this as a family) with flour. If using *Springerle* moulds, break off a small piece of dough and roll it out to about 7mm/¼in thick and roughly the size of your chosen mould, then dust the top of the dough with flour again: it's important to make sure the whole piece of dough has a light dusting as this will prevent it from sticking in the mould. Place your mould onto the dough and press down gently to emboss the pattern on. Using a sharp knife, cut around the edge of the mould to trim off any excess bits of dough. Remove the

mould and gently lift the biscuit onto a prepared baking sheet. Repeat this process until all of the dough is used up (re-rolling any offcuts), arranging the biscuits 2cm/¾in apart to allow room for expansion.

If using mooncake or maamoul cookie moulds, break off a small piece of dough, dust it all over with flour and then press it into your selected mould, flattening the bottom of the dough with the palm of your hand, then tip the mould over and bang it gently on the work surface, holding one hand underneath it to catch the dough as the biscuit is released. Gently lay the biscuit on a prepared baking sheet and trim the rough edges off with a sharp knife. Repeat this process until all of the dough is used up (re-rolling any offcuts), arranging the biscuits 2cm/¾in apart.

If using cookie cutters, simply roll out the dough on a lightly floured work surface to 7mm/¼in, cut out festive shapes and gently lay on the prepared sheets, as above. Re-roll the dough offcuts into more biscuits.

Leave the sheets uncovered overnight, or anywhere between 12–24 hours, to air dry.

When you are ready to bake the *Springerle*, heat the oven to 160°C/140°C fan/320°F. Bake the biscuits for about 25 minutes until firm to the touch; they should remain as pale as possible, so check them after 15 minutes – if they seem to be browning a little, cover with baking parchment for the remainder of the baking time.

Transfer to a wire rack to cool completely. Stored in an airtight container, they will keep well for up to 2 months. The longer they are stored, the crunchier and harder they'll become.

Pictured overleaf / baked biscuits pictured on pages 57 and 75

Nussplätzchen

NUT BISCUITS

Nut biscuits are very popular around Advent and Christmas time in Germany and, generally speaking, they keep well for a long time so are baked during the first half of December.

Almonds, hazelnuts and walnuts are intrinsically linked with Advent, just as certain spices, like cinnamon, ginger and clove are. And while this chapter includes just five recipes, there are actually about 45 recipes in this book that are based around or include nuts.

I always try to include at least one nut biscuit on my Christmas *Bunter Teller*. During Advent I'm pretty relaxed about what goes onto the plate, not fussing too much if there are only three biscuit choices, or indeed if all the biscuits are of the same variety, such as all *Lebkuchen*, for example – there are so many different kinds of *Lebkuchen* that I feel they are varied enough in themselves. But on Christmas Eve I go all out and make the Queen of *Bunter Teller*, with as many flavours, varieties, textures and shapes as possible – for Germans Christmas Eve is, after all, the pinnacle of the festive celebrations.

Florentiner
Cherry and almond Florentines

MAKES ABOUT 16

These are, along with the hazelnut macaroons, one of the more elegant biscuits in the book. Usually they aren't part of my Bunter Teller, instead I like to serve them on a plate all of their own. More for after dinner than with tea in the afternoon, I'd say, but of course it's up to you.

They make a really special Christmas gift boxed up and tied with a ribbon, but quite frankly I'd be happy to receive them in a Tupperware box – it's the thought that counts, as they say, and these are very thoughtful.

They are quite odd to bake compared to any other kind of biscuit – high in butter and low in flour, it seems like they won't work. The method does take some getting used to, and for this reason it's good to only bake one sheet at a time, but if you stick to it you'll be successful.

50g (3½ tbsp) unsalted butter, at room temp
80g (6½ tbsp) soft light brown sugar
2 tbsp plain (all-purpose) flour
80g (3oz) flaked (slivered) almonds

50g (1¾oz) glacé cherries, roughly chopped
30g (1oz) mixed peel
Pinch of fine sea salt

FOR THE BASE
100g (3½oz) dark chocolate
¼ tsp coconut oil

Heat the oven to 180°C/160°C fan/350°F and line 3 large baking sheets with non-stick baking parchment.

In a medium bowl, cream the butter and sugar together with a wooden spoon until light and fluffy, then add the remaining ingredients and gently mix through.

Using a teaspoon, spoon small amounts of the mixture onto the prepared sheets, placing them at least 10cm/4in apart. It's quite a sturdy mix and so will just sit there in a lump, and this is fine and how it's supposed to be – I usually find that they spread to roughly 7cm /2¾in in diameter, so 6 is the maximum one sheet can hold.

Bake for about 10 minutes, taking the sheet out after 5 minutes and flattening the centre of the Florentines slightly with the back of a teaspoon. After the full cooking time, they will have spread further and will need gentle re-shaping around the edges while still warm on the sheet. Allow to cool completely on the sheet, then transfer, flipped upside down, to a wire rack.

Put the chocolate and coconut oil into a heatproof bowl. Place the bowl over a small saucepan with a 1cm/⅜in depth of water in the bottom. Turn the heat on low and wait for the chocolate to melt. Once the chocolate starts melting, stir it so that the coconut oil is evenly dispersed. Take off the heat once the chocolate is glossy and fluid.

Spoon a teaspoonful of the melted chocolate onto the base of each Florentine, spreading it almost to the edges with the back of a teaspoon. Allow to set for 10 minutes before dragging a fork through the chocolate in squiggly patterns – this is purely for looks and is a step that can be left out. It will take an hour or so for the chocolate to set fully.

Stored in an airtight container, these will keep well for around a week.

Nussstangen
Nut batons

MAKES ABOUT 40

Nussstangen are a classic butter-rich nut biscuit – this version is loosely based on Heidesand (shortbread) made with icing sugar instead of granulated or caster, giving them an extra-smooth texture. If you prefer a crunchier biscuit you could also make Nußtangen using Vanillespritzgebäck dough (see page 104). I prefer to make these with ground almonds and ground hazelnuts for a real depth of nut flavour, but you can experiment with other ground nuts too, such as walnut or pistachio; it all just comes down to personal taste.

150g (1 cup plus 2 tbsp) plain (all-purpose) flour
50g (½ cup minus 1 tbsp) ground almonds (almond flour)
50g (1¾oz) hazelnuts, blanched and ground
Pinch of fine sea salt
125g (½ cup plus 1 tbsp) unsalted butter, at room temp

90g (⅔ cup) icing (confectioners') sugar, plus extra for dusting
1 tsp vanilla extract

FOR THE TOPPING
1 egg, beaten
50g (1¾oz) blanched hazelnuts, finely chopped

Heat the oven to 200°C/180°C fan/400°F and line two baking sheets with non-stick baking parchment.

Put the flour, ground almonds, ground hazelnuts and salt into a large mixing bowl. Add the butter and gently work it into the dry ingredients with your fingertips until it resembles something similar to breadcrumbs. Now add the icing sugar and mix through so it's evenly dispersed. Spoon in the vanilla extract and bring the dough together with your hands. Knead for about 3 minutes until a soft, pliable dough is formed. (Alternatively, put all the ingredients into a free-standing electric mixer fitted with a paddle attachment and beat everything to a pliable dough on a low speed for a couple of minutes.)

Split the dough into two equal parts. Dust the work surface with icing sugar and roll out one half of the dough to a 5mm/⅛in thickness. Using a sharp knife, cut out rectangles about 6 × 2cm/2½ × ¾in. Lay them on the prepared baking sheets with care, leaving about a 2cm/¾in gap between each. Repeat this process with the remaining dough.

Brush the top of each biscuit with the beaten egg then sprinkle each one with some chopped nuts – you can be quite liberal here and it doesn't matter if the nuts pile up a bit because the biscuits do spread a little.

Bake in the oven for about 10 minutes until golden brown.

Allow to cool on the sheets for a minute before transferring to a wire rack to cool completely. Stored in an airtight container, these will last for a good 3 weeks.

Haselnusskipferl
Hazelnut crescents

MAKES ABOUT 50

These are the nutty, more edgy sibling to the classic Vanillekipferl *(see page 202).*

170g (1¼ cups) plain
   (all-purpose) flour
10g (⅓oz) unsweetened
   cocoa powder
Pinch of fine sea salt
80g (3oz) hazelnuts,
   blanched and ground
125g (½ cup plus
   1 tbsp) unsalted
   butter, at room temp

75g (½ cup plus ½ tbsp)
   icing (confectioners')
   sugar, plus extra for
   dusting
1 egg yolk
1 tsp vanilla extract

Put the flour, cocoa powder, salt and ground hazelnuts into a large mixing bowl. Add the butter and gently work it into the dry ingredients with your fingertips until it resembles something similar to breadcrumbs. Now add the icing sugar and mix through so it's evenly dispersed. Add the egg yolk and vanilla extract. Bring the dough together with your hands and knead for about 3 minutes until a soft, pliable dough is formed. (Alternatively, put all the ingredients into a free-standing electric mixer fitted with a paddle attachment and beat everything to a pliable dough on a low speed for a couple of minutes.) Form the dough into a ball, wrap and refrigerate for 1 hour.

Heat the oven to 180°C/160°C fan/350°F and line two baking sheets with non-stick baking parchment.

Take a small, teaspoon-sized piece of dough and roll into a little sausage, 5cm/2in long with tapered edges. Form into a crescent shape and place gently on a baking sheet. Repeat until all of the dough is used up.

Bake in the oven for about 12 minutes until just starting to colour.

Remove from the sheet and transfer to a wire rack. While still hot, sift icing sugar liberally over the biscuits. Once completely cool, store in an airtight container where they will keep for a good 3 weeks.

Mandelhörnchen
Almond and marzipan crescents

MAKES ABOUT 40

Mandelhörnchen are an all-year-round classic German biscuit, so firmly seated in the nation's heart that they would be sorely missed if they were excluded from Advent celebrations. For me, more than anything, it's their crescent shape that makes them particularly festive and they sit comfortably among the other Kipferl *variety of biscuits on a* Bunter Teller.

The main ingredient for Mandelhörnchen *in Germany is usually* Marzipanrohmasse, *but I've tested and written this recipe using marzipan, which gives them a uniquely chewy texture and subtle almond flavour, which I prefer. Often they are also made with added almond extract but I don't feel the need to include it as the toasty flaked almonds on the outside of the biscuits are flavour enough. It's custom to dip each end in chocolate but more often than not I don't bother, preferring to let the almonds do the talking.*

175g (6oz) flaked (slivered) almonds
500g (1lb 2oz) marzipan, grated (I prefer to use golden for colour, but white is also fine)
300g (2⅓ cups) ground almonds (almond flour)

200g (1½ cups minus 1 tbsp) icing (confectioners') sugar
3 egg whites

FOR DIPPING
200g (7oz) dark chocolate
¼ tsp coconut oil

Heat the oven to 150°C/130°C fan/300°F and line 3 large baking sheets with non-stick baking parchment. Put the flaked almonds into a shallow dish.

Put the grated marzipan, ground almonds, icing sugar and egg whites into a large bowl. Mix with a wooden spoon, then use your hands to knead it into a dough. It will be very sticky and messy.

Pinch off a walnut-sized piece of dough and roll between your hands to form a log about 9cm/3½in long. Roll in the flaked almonds until coated all over, then bend into a crescent shape and place it gently onto a prepared sheet.

Repeat until all of the dough is used up. If it becomes too sticky, you can dust your hands with a little icing sugar to help the rolling process – just remember the aim is for the almonds to stick and too much icing sugar will prevent that from happening.

Bake in the oven for about 18 minutes until just golden. Allow to cool on the sheets for a minute before transferring to a wire rack to cool completely.

Meanwhile, if you choose to dip them in chocolate as per tradition, put the chocolate and coconut oil into a heatproof bowl placed over a small saucepan with a 1cm/⅜in depth of water in the bottom. Turn the heat on low and wait for the chocolate to melt. Once melted, stir it until glossy and fluid.

Dip each end of the crescents into the chocolate, or spoon it over instead (which I find easier when you're coming to the end of the chocolate). Lay the biscuits back down onto the wire rack and allow the chocolate an hour or so to set.

Stored in an airtight container, these will last for at least 3 weeks.

Pictured overleaf

Haselnuss-Zitronenherzen
Hazelnut and lemon hearts

These biscuits came by way of our late next-door neighbour Helga. It was pure chance that another German happened to buy the house next door to my parents in Wales, and as luck would have it Helga didn't bake the same Advent Plätzchen as us. Between both houses we really covered a broad Gebäck spectrum.

Hazelnut hearts are soft in texture and have a lovely balance of sweet and sour with a pleasant contrast between earthy toasted nuts and refreshing lemon tang. I think of them as the sister to Zimtsterne.

2 egg whites
180g (1 cup minus 1½ tbsp) soft light brown sugar
2 tsp ground cinnamon
Pinch of fine sea salt
Finely grated zest of 1 lemon
300g (10½oz) hazelnuts, blanched and ground

60g (7 tbsp) plain (all-purpose) flour
½ tsp baking powder

FOR THE ICING
140g (1 cup) icing (confectioners') sugar, sifted, plus extra for dusting
2 tbsp lemon juice

Heat the oven to 180°C/160°C fan/350°F and line two large baking sheets with non-stick baking parchment.

Put the egg whites into the bowl of a free-standing electric mixer fitted with a whisk attachment (or use a large mixing bowl and a hand-held electric whisk), and whisk for a few minutes on high speed until stiff peaks form.

Turn the speed down and add the sugar one tablespoon at a time, whisking all the while until it is all incorporated and you have a glossy meringue. Now add the cinnamon, salt and lemon zest and whisk for a further few seconds.

Mix the ground hazelnuts, flour and baking powder together in a bowl until evenly combined. Using a wooden spoon, fold the nut mixture into the meringue. The dough will become quite stiff, at which point you may need to use your hands to bring it together into a ball.

Dust the work surface with icing sugar. Separate the dough into two halves and roll one half out to a 5mm/⅛in thickness. Cut out biscuits using a heart-shaped cookie cutter (see pages 258–9) and place on the prepared baking sheets, leaving 2cm/¾in between each to allow for a little spreading. Repeat with the other half of the dough, then re-roll all the dough offcuts into more biscuits.

Bake for 12–15 minutes until firm to the touch but not brown; they should still be soft when bitten into. Allow to cool on the sheets for a couple of minutes before transferring to a wire rack to cool completely.

Meanwhile, make the icing by mixing the icing sugar and lemon juice together in a bowl until glossy and smooth.

Ice the top of each cooled biscuit, using a small knife to ensure the icing comes right to the edges. Leave on the wire rack for an hour or so to air dry and fully set.

Stored in an airtight container, these will last for up to a month.

Schokoladenplätzchen

CHOCOLATE BISCUITS

If ever there were a time of year where chocolate is consumed like there's no tomorrow, Christmas (and, OK, Easter too) is it. It's for this reason that I shy away from too many chocolate biscuits in Advent baking. As it is, so many *Weihnachtsplätzchen* are finished off with chocolate, either by being dipped into it or with it drizzled on top. So, it's with this in mind that I've kept this chapter short and sweet – just three of the best.

Quite often too, chocolate biscuits are a vehicle for using up all the leftover, half-eaten or broken chocolate Santas and reindeer from *Nikolaus*. The nut biscuit chapter and this chocolate biscuit chapter have a lot in common in the sense that both are short, yet could in fact contain thousands of biscuit varieties. If you are looking for more recipes that include chocolate, turn to the Christmas confections (page 218) or marzipan sweets (228) chapters.

Schwarz-Weiß-Gebäck
Chocolate and vanilla shortbreads

MAKES 40–45

I have always been fond of Schwarz-Weiß Gebäck, it's just so pleasing in every way. Almost like eating two biscuits, one chocolate and one vanilla, in one. Part of the joy in making these crisp buttery biscuits is that you can let your creativity run wild – chequer the dough, swirl it into pinwheels, marble it or make it stripy. I find that pinwheels or stripes are the easiest patterns, certainly so if you have children helping. For a bit of fun you can also create lollipops out of the pinwheel version by baking wooden sticks into them.

200g (1½ cups) plain (all-purpose) flour
50g (⅓ cup) cornflour (cornstarch)
175g (¾ cup) unsalted butter, at room temp
Pinch of fine sea salt
50g (¼ cup) caster (superfine) sugar

50g (6 tbsp) icing (confectioners') sugar, plus extra for dusting
1 tsp vanilla extract
25g (1oz) unsweetened cocoa powder
Milk, for assembling

Put the flour, cornflour, butter and salt in a mixing bowl and rub the butter into the flour with your fingertips until it becomes the consistency of fine breadcrumbs. Add the sugars and vanilla extract and, using your hands, bring it all together into a dough. (Alternatively, which I find much easier, put all the ingredients except the cocoa powder and milk into the bowl of a free-standing electric mixer fitted with a paddle attachment, and beat on a medium speed until everything comes together into a ball of dough.)

Split the dough in two. Place one half to the side on the surface and keep one half in the bowl. Add the cocoa powder to the dough in the bowl and knead it in with your hands until evenly incorporated.

Now comes the fun part of choosing which pattern you want to go with – I'll start with the easiest first, working up to the most tricky.

Lightly dust the work surface with icing sugar to stop the dough from sticking to it.

MARBLING

Roll both pieces of dough into a log about 30cm/12in long. Twist both pieces together and then gently collapse it into a ball and knead the dough for 10 seconds. Form it back into a round log of about 30cm long.

PINWHEELING

Roll the vanilla dough into a rectangle shape of 30cm/12in long. Do the same with the cocoa dough. Brush the vanilla dough with milk and carefully lift the cocoa dough up, supporting it with your hands underneath, and place it on top of the vanilla dough. Brush the top with milk again. Starting with a long end closest to you, roll the dough up away from you into a tight log shape. *(Pictured on page 2.)*

STRIPES

Follow the same steps as per the pinwheeling but instead of rolling the dough up, cut it lengthwise into three equal parts. Brush one with milk and place one strip on top of this, pressing down gently so it sticks properly. Now brush the top of this with milk and add the remaining strip, pressing down gently again so that it sticks properly.

CHEQUERED

Follow the same steps as per the stripes, but instead of cutting the dough lengthwise into three equal parts, cut it lengthwise into strips 1cm/³⁄₈in wide. Using milk to sandwich the strips together, create a chequered pattern until all the dough is used up – these can be either rectangular or square in shape, totally up to you. (*Pictured on page 34.*)

Cover the dough and refrigerate for 30 minutes. Heat the oven to 180°C/160°C fan/350°F and line two baking sheets with non-stick baking parchment.

Lay the dough on the work surface and cut it into slices 5mm/⅛in thick. Place on the baking sheets, leaving 1cm/³⁄₈in between each for spreading. Don't worry if the shapes come apart a little on slicing, just push each biscuit together gently while it's on the sheet; as it bakes it will meld together.

Bake for about 12 minutes until firm to the touch but not browned. Allow to cool on the sheet for 2 minutes before transferring to a wire rack to cool completely.

Stored in an airtight container, these will keep well for 3 weeks.

Schokopfefferminztaler
Chocolate peppermint biscuits

MAKES ABOUT 25

I grew up with After-Eights at Christmas time, thinking they were the height of sophistication, as did many other children (possibly adults too) of the 1980s. This is my biscuit ode to them, with a tooth-achingly sweet peppermint icing.

200g (1½ cups) plain (all-purpose) flour
25g (1oz) unsweetened cocoa powder
Pinch of fine sea salt
150g (⅔ cup) unsalted butter, at room temp
80g (6½ tbsp) dark brown sugar

FOR THE TOPPING
100g (¾ cup minus ½ tbsp) icing (confectioners') sugar, sifted, plus extra for dusting
1 tsp peppermint extract
1 tbsp water
Chocolate sprinkles, to decorate

Heat the oven to 180°C/160°C fan/350°F and line a large baking sheet (or two) with non-stick baking parchment.

Put the flour, cocoa powder and salt into a mixing bowl and, using a wooden spoon, mix thoroughly. Now add the butter and rub it in with your fingertips until it resembles fine breadcrumbs. Add the sugar and use your hands to bring it all together into a dough. (Alternatively, put all the ingredients into the bowl of a free-standing electric mixer fitted with a paddle attachment and beat on a medium speed until everything comes together into a ball of dough.)

Dust the work surface with icing sugar and roll the dough out to 5mm/⅛in thick. Cut out biscuits using any shaped cookie cutters – I like to keep mine quite small, sort of two-bite-sized (see pages 258–9). Place on the prepared baking sheet(s), leaving 1cm/⅜in between each one. Re-roll the dough offcuts into more biscuits.

Bake in the oven for about 12 minutes until firm to the touch. Leave to cool on the sheet(s) for a minute or two, then transfer to a wire rack to cool completely.

Once the biscuits are cool, mix the icing sugar, peppermint extract and water together in a small bowl until glossy and smooth. Using a teaspoon, put small amounts (½ teaspoon) of icing into the centre of the biscuit and gently spread it out until just short of the edges. Sprinkle each one with chocolate sprinkles. Allow the icing to set, for about 1–2 hours, before storing in an airtight container, where they will keep well for 2 weeks. They will be very crisp at first, but will soften over time.

Basler Brunsli
Spiced chocolate hearts

MAKES ABOUT 50

Basler Brunsli are a Swiss import, and one that Germans have adopted with open arms. It's only the name that gives away their birthplace and original home of Basel. Made with chocolate that has been ground or grated into a coarse sand-like texture and baked on a layer of demerara sugar, these biscuits are both chewy and crunchy all in one.

They are traditionally made with Kirsch, *which gives a sharp, fruity undertone, but I actually prefer them made with brandy (or even cherry brandy).*

The dough is quite crumbly and isn't the easiest to work with, but it's forgiving too; if it tears a little on rolling just press it back together again. They aren't the prettiest of biscuits once baked anyway, which takes the pressure off somewhat. What they lack in looks, though, they make up for in flavour.

200g (7oz) dark chocolate (50–70% cocoa solids)
250g (2¼ cups) ground almonds (almond flour)
75g (6 tbsp) soft light brown sugar
½ tsp ground cinnamon
1 tbsp brandy or *Kirsch*
2 egg whites
Pinch of fine sea salt
About 2 tbsp demerara sugar
Icing (confectioners') sugar, if needed

Heat the oven to 150°C/130°C fan/300°F and line two baking sheets with non-stick baking parchment.

I tend to make these in the food processor for ease. Break the chocolate into pieces and blitz in the processor for about 2 minutes until the consistency of coarse sand – I sometimes find it helps to pulse it near the end. Now add all the remaining ingredients except the demerara sugar and blitz for a further minute or so until it all comes together as a dough.

If you are making these by hand, grate the chocolate using a box grater (coarse is fine as chocolate isn't like cheese, it will still end up being a fine-ish rubble). Add the remaining ingredients except the demerara sugar and mix together with your hands until it comes together into a ball.

Divide the dough in half and sprinkle the work surface liberally with demerara sugar. Place the dough on top of the sugar and roll it out to a 1cm/⅜in thickness. If the rolling pin is sticking too much, dust the top lightly with icing sugar. Using a cookie cutter (see pages 258–9), cut out little heart shapes and place on the prepared baking sheets with 1cm/⅜in between each (these don't spread much at all). Repeat with the remaining dough, and re-roll all the dough offcuts into more biscuits.

Bake in the oven for 15–18 minutes until they feel dry-ish to the touch; they will still be very soft, and this is normal – once out of the oven and cooled they will firm up a lot. Leave to cool on the sheets for a minute or two, then transfer to a wire rack and allow to cool completely.

Stored in an airtight container, these will keep well for a good month.

Also pictured: Weiße Pfeffernüsse *(p.117),* Mandelhörnchen *(p.131),* Schokopfefferminztaler *(p.140)*

13

Makronen

MACAROONS

I could say this for every chapter, I know, but I really mean it with a passion when I say that I could have written an entire book on macaroons alone. Macaroons add a bit of light relief from the honey-heavy spiced doughs and butter-rich biscuits that make up German Advent baking. They aren't just light in texture, but are light in temperament too, adding a bit of fun to an otherwise to-be-taken-seriously topic. Light like clouds with a warmly toasted flavour, it's easy to see why coconut macaroons are one of the favourites to appear at Christmas time. And they have a magic trick up their sleeve, too,

for they can morph themselves from snowballs into snowy mountains with chocolate caps — take your pick.

Macaroons are one of the easiest things to make (provided you have an electric whisk, otherwise they'd actually be one of the most arduous) and tick all the boxes in terms of festive spirit. Imagine the look on your friend's face when you show up at their house holding a box of snowball macaroons tied up with a glossy red ribbon, or indeed the feeling of opening up the door to such a thing yourself. You won't regret making macaroons this Christmas.

Kokosmakronen
Coconut macaroons

MAKES 25–30

These are the stuff that winter dreams are made of. As a child I spent ages imagining that fantasy lands made out of coconut mountains with chocolate snow really might exist. And in some way Advent magically did bring this whimsical place to life in our kitchen. It's hard for me to visualize a better world than one where the houses are made of gingerbread and the stars of cinnamon-spiced dough, try as I may.

2 egg whites
100g (½ cup plus
  1 tbsp) caster
  (superfine) sugar
Pinch of fine sea salt
1 tsp vanilla extract
150g (5oz) desiccated
  (dried shredded)
  coconut

FOR THE 'SNOW CAPS'
80g (3oz) dark
  chocolate, broken into
  chunks
¼ tsp coconut oil

Heat the oven to 155°C/135°C fan/310°F and line a large baking sheet with non-stick baking parchment.

Put the egg whites into the bowl of a free-standing electric mixer fitted with a whisk attachment (or use a mixing bowl and electric hand-held whisk) and whisk for a couple of minutes on a high speed until stiff peaks form. Turn the speed down and add the sugar one tablespoon at a time, whisking all the while, until it is all incorporated and you have a glossy meringue. Now add the salt and vanilla extract and whisk for a further couple of seconds. Using a large metal spoon, gently fold the coconut into the meringue.

Spoon heaped teaspoons of the mixture 2cm/¾in apart onto the prepared baking sheet.

With your free hand, pinch the tops of the little mounds to create peaks (the idea is that they should look like mini mountains). If you are making the snowball variety then there is no need to pinch the tops; instead use the spoon to make the macaroons as round as possible.

Bake in the oven for 25–30 minutes. The idea is more that they dry out than bake as such. They will turn oaty in colour, but you don't want them to turn golden or brown. Leave to cool on the sheet for a few minutes, then transfer to a wire rack to cool completely.

Put the chocolate and coconut oil into a heatproof bowl and place the bowl over a small saucepan with a 1cm/⅜in depth of water in the bottom. Turn the heat on low and wait for the chocolate to melt. Once it starts melting, stir so that the coconut oil is evenly dispersed. Take off the heat once the chocolate is glossy and fluid.

Spoon the chocolate onto the peaks of each mountain to create little 'snow caps'. The chocolate will take an hour or so to set properly so don't box the macaroons up until then.

Stored in an airtight container, these will keep well for at least 3 weeks.

Haselnussmakronen
Hazelnut macaroons

MAKES ABOUT 50

Hazelnut macaroons, otherwise known as 'Nutella biscuits' in our house, are very, very moreish. One of the more elegant biscuits in this book, these would be lovely with a small coffee as the final round after a festive dinner.

Blanched hazelnuts are easy enough to find in supermarkets, but you may struggle to get hold of ground ones. I use a coffee grinder to grind mine at home.

2 egg whites
180g (1 cup minus 1½ tbsp) soft light brown sugar
Pinch of fine sea salt
250g (9oz) blanched hazelnuts, ground

2 level tbsp cornflour (cornstarch)
100g (3½oz) dark chocolate (at least 50% cocoa solids), broken into pieces

Heat the oven to 160°C/140°C fan/320°F and line two large baking sheets with non-stick baking parchment.

Put the egg whites into the bowl of a free-standing electric mixer fitted with a whisk attachment (or use a mixing bowl and electric hand-held whisk) and whisk for a couple of minutes on a high speed until stiff peaks form. Turn the speed down and add the sugar one tablespoon at a time, whisking all the while, until it is all incorporated and you have a glossy meringue. Now add the salt and whisk for a further couple of seconds.

Mix the ground hazelnuts and cornflour together in a bowl. Add half of this nut mixture to the meringue and fold it in gently using a large, metal spoon, trying not to knock out too much air. Once it's been incorporated, add the remaining half and repeat the process.

Spoon the macaroon mixture into a piping bag with a 1cm/⅜in opening or nozzle. (Alternatively, use a plastic freezer bag, which you have snipped the corner off to leave a 1cm/⅜in opening.)

Pipe logs about 6cm/2½in long onto the sheets, spaced 3cm/1¼in apart to allow for spreading. Bake in the oven for about 20 minutes until firm to the touch. Let the macaroons cool on the baking sheet.

Meanwhile, put the chocolate into a heatproof bowl. Place this bowl over a small saucepan with a 1cm/⅜in depth of water in the bottom. Turn the heat on low and wait for the chocolate to melt. Once it starts melting, stir it so that it melts evenly. Take off the heat once the chocolate is glossy and fluid.

Pour the chocolate into a piping bag with a small icing nozzle and drizzle it over each cooled macaroon. (Alternatively, use a teaspoon and move it swiftly over the sheet of macaroons – this creates more of an 'organic' uneven drizzle.)

Allow the chocolate to set – this will take at least an hour – before storing in an airtight container, where they will keep well for up to 4 weeks.

Dattel-Walnuss-Makronen
Date and walnut macaroons

MAKES ABOUT 55

While date and walnut macaroons may sound a little dowdy or even 'worthy', they are anything but. Rich and toffee-like, with a chewy bite, these rather unassuming-looking macaroons are pretty special, with a hint of old-fashioned Christmas about them.

2 egg whites
180g (1 cup minus 1½ tbsp) soft light brown sugar
Pinch of fine sea salt
1 tsp vanilla extract
100g (3½oz) pitted dates, finely chopped (not Medjool, just regular dates)

100g (3½oz) walnuts, finely chopped
1 tbsp cornflour (cornstarch)
Small walnut pieces, to decorate

Heat the oven to 160°C/140°C fan/320°F and line two large baking sheets with non-stick baking parchment.

Put the egg whites into the bowl of a free-standing electric mixer fitted with a whisk attachment (or use a mixing bowl and electric hand-held whisk) and whisk for a couple of minutes on a high speed until stiff peaks form. Turn the speed down and add the sugar one tablespoon at a time, whisking all the while, until it is all incorporated and you have a glossy meringue. Now add the salt and vanilla extract and whisk for a further couple of seconds.

Mix the dates, walnuts and cornflour together in a bowl. Add half of this nut mixture to the meringue and fold it in gently using a large metal spoon, trying not to knock out too much air. Once it's been incorporated evenly, add the remaining half and repeat the process.

Scoop out small teaspoons of the mixture and drop them gently onto the prepared sheets, spacing them 3cm/1¼in apart. Place a small walnut piece on top of each.

Bake in the oven for about 18 minutes until firm to the touch. Allow to cool on the sheet for a few minutes before transferring to a wire rack to cool completely.

Stored in an airtight container, these will keep well for 3 weeks or more, but will soften a little over time.

Schokoküsschen
Chocolate kisses

MAKES 60–70

Our boys love these bite-sized treats and they're a firm lunch box favourite throughout the year as well as on our Bunter Teller at Christmas time. I'm not entirely sure whether they fall into the meringue or macaroon camp, as they're a bit of both really. The idea for these came about from a classic German biscuit called Russisch Brot, which are little alphabet cookies beloved by children of kindergarten and primary school age. I often find the letters fiddly to pipe out and so came round to piping chocolate kisses – as I affectionately name them – instead.

2 egg whites
90g (7½ tbsp) soft light
  brown sugar
Pinch of fine sea salt
½ tsp vanilla extract
2 tbsp unsweetened
  cocoa powder
½ tsp ground cinnamon
1 tbsp cornflour
  (cornstarch)
1 tbsp plain (all-
  purpose) flour

Heat the oven to 180°C/160°C fan/350°F and line a large baking sheet with non-stick baking parchment (I squish my macaroons all onto one but you can use two if that's easier).

Put the egg whites into the bowl of a free-standing electric mixer fitted with a whisk attachment (or use a mixing bowl and electric hand-held whisk) and whisk for a couple of minutes on a high speed until stiff peaks form. Turn the speed down and add the sugar one tablespoon at a time, whisking all the while, until it is all incorporated and you have a glossy meringue. Now add the salt and vanilla extract and whisk for a further couple of seconds before adding the remaining ingredients. Whisk for a final 30 seconds so the flour and spices are incorporated.

Spoon the mixture into a piping bag fitted with a 1cm/⅜in star-shaped nozzle. (Alternatively, use a plastic freezer bag, which you have snipped the corner off to leave a 1cm/⅜in opening.)

Pipe little peaks of 1.5cm/½in diameter onto the sheet; they don't spread all that much so you only need a little space in between each one.

Bake in the oven for 15–18 minutes until firm to the touch but not browned. Cocoa powder does have a tendency to burn easily, so make sure you check them after 15 minutes. The longer you leave them in the oven the crisper they will be.

Allow to cool completely on the sheet before storing in an airtight container, where they will keep well for up to a month.

Doppeldecker

LAYERED BISCUITS

Layered biscuits, often with a cut-out centre, are one of the biscuits (cookies) that bring colour to a *Bunter Teller*. Usually a red jam (jelly) is used to sandwich the two biscuit halves together, which shines through the middle like a pane of stained glass. The jam softens and moistens the biscuits and the longer you keep them, the more melt-in-your-mouth they become. The top layer is more often than not dusted with icing (confectioners') sugar or frosted with a thin sugar glaze.

Probably the most universally well known of these Advent biscuits is the *Linzer* biscuit – an Austrian classic that has been adopted in many German households. Like *Lebkuchen*, though, the varieties of layered, jam-sandwiched biscuits are seemingly endless. In the past I've

made many including *Tannenbäume* – teetering towers of stars in decreasing sizes, stacked up in the shape of mini Christmas trees dusted with icing sugar snow – beautiful but almost impossible to eat without dismantling first. Aside from the one exception of a gingerbread house, I don't really like to destroy what I'm eating before I eat it, which is why I now limit my layered biscuits to three tiers.

It's true to say that I've never eaten the same layered biscuit twice in different friends' houses. It seems they're a biscuit that people are loyal to, both in flavour and shape, and I find this a charming trait on a *Bunter Teller*. It's comforting too in a way to know that the same biscuits will be in the same houses again next year.

Doppeldecker
Jam-filled double deckers

MAKES 18–20

While my mama is an exceptionally good home cook, biscuits aren't really her favourite thing to make and I didn't get my love of Advent baking from her. I learned about the magic of Adventsgebäck *as a small child from Omi, her mother, who took it upon herself to teach me all that she knew, filling the German biscuit void in our Welsh household. Later, during my early teenage years, and much to everyone's delight, I baked my way through countless German baking books during Advent, adding to the knowledge Omi had passed on.*

The one exception to mama's Christmas baking was Doppeldecker, *buttery biscuits filled with jam and a heart (or star) cut of out the centre; Germany's answer to the jammy dodger. These she baked every December without fail because they were my brother's favourite. I happily made up for the rest of the biscuits on the* Bunter Teller.

Made with apricot jam instead of raspberry, these are called Marillenringe *and are an Austrian Advent speciality. Also, if you switch the cut-out heart for three small circles they become* Pfauenaugen, *which means 'peacock eyes'.*

350g (2⅔ cups) plain (all-purpose) flour, plus extra for dusting
¼ tsp baking powder
Pinch of fine sea salt
125g (½ cup plus 1 tbsp) unsalted butter, at room temp

180g (1 cup) caster (superfine) sugar
1 tsp vanilla extract
1 egg, plus 1 egg yolk

TO ASSEMBLE AND FINISH
Raspberry jam (jelly)
Icing (confectioners') sugar, for dusting

Heat the oven to 200°C/180°C fan/400°F and line two large baking sheets with non-stick baking parchment.

Put the flour, baking powder and salt into a large mixing bowl. Add the butter and work it into the flour using your fingertips until it resembles breadcrumbs. Add the sugar and vanilla extract and mix through. Now add the egg and extra yolk and knead into a stiff dough. (Alternatively, put all the ingredients into the bowl of a free-standing electric mixer fitted with a paddle attachment, and beat until they come together as a stiff dough.)

Lightly dust the work surface with flour. Divide the dough in half and roll one half out to a 5mm/⅛in thickness. Cut out small rounds using a fluted cutter (see pages 258–9). Lay these on one of the baking sheets. Repeat with the other half of dough, laying the rounds on the second baking sheet. Use a smaller star- or heart-shaped cutter to cut out a shape from the centre of half of the rounds. (You can either place these small cut-out shapes on another lined baking sheet and bake them after the *Doppeldecker*, or simply roll them up into a ball of dough with all the offcuts and continue making the larger biscuits.)

Bake for about 10 minutes until lightly golden brown. Transfer the biscuits to two wire racks, one for the whole biscuits and one for the cut-out biscuits, to cool completely.

Once cool, spoon about ½ teaspoon of jam onto each whole biscuit. Dust each cut-out biscuit with icing sugar and gently lay one on top of each jam-covered biscuit. Stored in an airtight tin, these will keep for at least 3 weeks.

Terrassenplätzchen
Tiered star biscuits

MAKES ABOUT 25

Delicate, buttery, almond biscuits are sandwiched together
with golden apricot jam to make these tiered stars.

150g (1 cup plus
  2 tbsp) plain
  (all-purpose) flour
12g (1½ tbsp) cornflour
  (cornstarch)
50g (½ cup minus
  1 tbsp) ground
  almonds (almond
  flour)
Pinch of fine sea salt
125g (½ cup plus
  1 tbsp) unsalted
  butter, at room temp
100g (½ cup plus
  1 tbsp) caster
  (superfine) sugar
1 egg yolk

TO ASSEMBLE
AND FINISH
Apricot jam (jelly)
Icing (confectioners')
  sugar, for dusting

You will need 3
  different-sized
  star-shaped cutters
  (see pages 258–9).

Heat the oven to 200°C/180°C fan/400°F and line two large baking sheets with non-stick baking parchment.

Put both flours, the ground almonds and salt into a large mixing bowl. Add the butter and gently work it into the dry ingredients with your fingertips until it resembles something similar to breadcrumbs. Now add the sugar and egg yolk and bring the dough together with your hands. Knead for about 3 minutes until a soft, pliable dough is formed. (Alternatively, put all the ingredients into the bowl of a free-standing electric mixer fitted with a paddle attachment, and beat together to a pliable dough.)

Dust the work surface with icing sugar. Roll out the dough to a thickness of 3mm/⅛in. Cut out 25 of each size of star shape, re-rolling the dough offcuts into more biscuits. Place on the prepared baking sheets and bake in the oven for about 8 minutes until golden. Leave to cool on the sheets for 1–2 minutes, then transfer to a wire rack to cool.

Once completely cooled, lay the largest stars out on a baking sheet. Spoon ½ teaspoon of apricot jam onto each one, then top with the middle-sized star. Spoon ¼ teaspoon onto this middle star and top with the smallest star. Dust the biscuits with icing sugar and store in an airtight container; they will keep well for around 2 weeks.

Linzer Plätzchen
Linzer biscuits

These are the biscuit version of a Linzer tart — an Austrian classic that originated, as its name suggests, in the town of Linz. Despite being made year round they have become synonymous with Christmas. Often they're made with ground almonds but I prefer the flavour of ground hazelnuts — ground walnuts would also work well here too. The cocoa powder in the dough isn't there to add a chocolatey flavour but rather to bring out the nuttiness of the hazelnuts and the warm notes of cinnamon.

175g (1⅓ cups) plain (all-purpose) flour
25g (3½ tbsp) cornflour (cornstarch)
100g (1 cup minus 1½ tbsp) hazelnuts, ground (or half hazelnut/half almond)
1 tsp unsweetened cocoa powder
½ tsp ground cinnamon
Pinch of fine sea salt
120g (½ cup plus 1 tsp) unsalted butter, at room temp

Finely grated zest of ½ lemon
120g (⅔ cup) caster (superfine) sugar
1 egg

TO ASSEMBLE AND FINISH
Icing (confectioners') sugar, for dusting
80g (3oz) raspberry or blackcurrant jam (jelly)

Line two large baking sheets with non-stick baking parchment.

Put both flours, the ground hazelnuts, cocoa powder, cinnamon and salt in a large mixing bowl. Add the butter and gently work it into the dry ingredients with your fingertips until it resembles something similar to breadcrumbs. Now add the lemon zest, sugar and egg and bring the dough together with your hands. Knead for about 3 minutes until a soft,

pliable dough is formed. (Alternatively, put all the ingredients into the bowl of a free-standing electric mixer fitted with a paddle attachment, and beat together to a pliable dough.)

Form the dough into a ball, wrap and refrigerate for 1 hour.

Heat the oven to 180°C/160°C fan/350°F.

Dust the work surface with icing sugar. Roll out the dough to a thickness of 5mm/⅛in. Cut out biscuits using a round cookie cutter (see pages 258–9) and lay them on the prepared baking sheets. Using a mini cutter, cut a smaller circle out of the centre of half the biscuits. Re-roll the dough offcuts into more biscuits.

Bake for about 10 minutes until just starting to turn golden. Transfer to two wire racks, one for the whole biscuits and one for the cut-out biscuits, to cool completely.

Once cool, spoon a generous ½ teaspoon of jam onto each whole biscuit. Dust each cut-out biscuit with icing sugar and gently lay one on top of each jam-covered biscuit. Stored in an airtight tin, these will keep for at least 3 weeks.

Kränze und Zöpfe

WREATHS AND PLAITS

While Advent is mainly about biscuits, it is also a time of year when soft, enriched yeasted cakes and breads come into their own. Christmas lends the perfect opportunity to get creative with form and shape by plaiting dough and studding it with jewelled fruit or creating wreaths of bread rolls to tear and share.

All of the breads in this chapter are light and are based around a classic *Rosinenzopf* (raisin plait), commonly eaten at breakfast or afternoon teatime (*Kaffee und Kuchen*). The white bread dough is usually enriched with

butter and eggs but I find adding *Quark* — a soft fresh curd cheese that is similar in texture to ricotta but with a sharp citrusy tang, making it closer to labneh or hung yogurt in flavour — works a treat in the dough and creates a light, fluffy crumb that I prefer.

I specify fresh yeast for these recipes but have also given quantities for dried yeast should you find fresh hard to get hold of. Dried will work, but the bread is much lighter with fresh yeast and it is preferable, so definitely worth seeking out, I feel.

Rosinenzopf
Braided raisin bread

This dough is plaited into a festive loaf, which is also very popular at Easter time. It's slightly sweet from the raisins, but my version doesn't contain any added sugar and so it's still savoury. Sliced thinly and buttered it's good with cheese — blue especially, but the most popular toppings are jam and honey.

I sometimes add a teaspoon of ground cinnamon and a pinch of ground cloves to the flour. This version is not so good with cheese, but delicious toasted and buttered the next day and reminiscent of a teacake. For an extra snowy touch at Christmas you can sprinkle the top with Hagelzucker (pearl sugar) before baking. At Easter I like to nestle coloured boiled eggs inside the hollows of the plait once the loaf is baked. Basically, it can be adapted to suit any occasion and is one of Germany's most popular celebratory breads.

If you want to sweeten and enrich the dough further, by all means add some sugar (I'd say 50g/¼ cup) to the flour and knead in 40g (3 tablespoons) of butter along with the Quark.

450g (3¼ cups) strong white bread flour, plus extra for dusting
½ tsp fine sea salt
20g (¾oz) fresh yeast, or 10g (⅓oz) dried
200ml (¾ cup plus 1½ tbsp) tepid whole milk
200g (1 cup minus 1 tbsp) Quark
80g (3oz) raisins
1 egg, beaten

Put the flour and salt into a large bowl and mix with a wooden spoon. Crumble the yeast (or sprinkle if using dried) into the tepid milk and stir to dissolve. Pour the yeasted milk into the flour mixture, add the *Quark* and, using your hands, bring the ingredients together into a rough dough. Tip the dough out onto a floured surface and knead for about 10 minutes until it becomes more elastic. Form it into a ball and nestle it into the bottom of the bowl. Cover the bowl with a tea towel and set aside in a warm spot to rise for about 1 hour, or until doubled in size. (Alternatively, put the flour and salt into the bowl of a free-standing electric mixer fitted with a dough hook, pour in the yeasted milk mixture, add the *Quark* and knead for 5–8 minutes until elastic. Cover and set aside, as above.)

Knock the dough back with your fist and add the raisins. Gently knead the dough so that the raisins are incorporated evenly throughout.

Line a large baking sheet with non-stick baking parchment and split the dough into three pieces. Sprinkle the work surface with water and, with wet hands, roll each piece of dough into a sausage shape about 40cm/16in long. Place all three pieces of dough on the prepared baking sheet and braid them together, tucking the ends in and underneath.

Cover the loaf with a tea towel and let it rise in a warm spot for about 30 minutes, or until the dough has visibly grown by at least half its size again. Heat the oven to 200°C/180°C fan/400°F.

Brush the top of the loaf with the beaten egg and bake for 25–30 minutes until rusty brown. To test if the loaf is done, tap the bottom with your knuckles; it should sound relatively hollow. If you think it needs more time you may need to cover the top with foil to avoid it burning.

Transfer to a wire rack to cool. It is best served still just warm the day it's baked, but if wrapped well it will keep for a further 2 days.

Weihnachtskranz
Christmas wreath

MAKES 1 LARGE WREATH, SERVES 8–10

This might well be the prettiest thing to have come out of our kitchen all year.

It has a light and fluffy, yet rich, moist and indulgent crumb. I know some of you might find glacé cherries a little too much, and you probably aren't wrong – aside from a handful of recipes, this one included, I'm inclined to agree. They are, after all, a shallow ingredient that's more about looks than taste.

450g (3¼ cups) strong white bread flour, plus extra for dusting
30g (2 tbsp) caster (superfine) sugar
½ tsp fine sea salt
1 tsp ground cinnamon
20g (¾oz) fresh yeast, or 10g (⅓oz) dried
180ml (¾ cup) tepid whole milk
200g (1 cup minus 1 tbsp) Quark
50g (3½ tbsp) unsalted butter, at room temp
1 tsp vanilla extract
Finely grated zest of 1 lemon
50g (1¾oz) raisins
60g (2oz) glacé cherries, chopped

30g (1oz) flaked (slivered) almonds, roughly chopped
1 egg, beaten

FOR THE GLAZE
100g (¾ cup minus ½ tbsp) icing (confectioners') sugar, sifted
1 tbsp lemon juice
2 tsp water

TO DECORATE
30g (1oz) glacé cherries, halved
30g (1oz) flaked (slivered) almonds, toasted

Put the flour, sugar, salt and cinnamon into a large bowl and mix with a wooden spoon. Crumble the yeast (or sprinkle if using dried) into the tepid milk and stir to dissolve. Pour the yeasted milk into the flour mixture, add the *Quark*, butter, vanilla extract and lemon zest and, using your hands, bring everything together into a rough dough. Tip out onto a floured surface and knead for 10 minutes until elastic. Form it into a ball and

nestle it into the bowl. Cover with a tea towel and set aside in a warm spot to rise for an hour, or until considerably risen in size. (Alternatively, put the flour, sugar, salt and cinnamon into the bowl of a free-standing electric mixer fitted with a dough hook, pour in the yeasted milk, add the *Quark*, butter, lemon zest and vanilla extract and knead for 5–8 minutes until elastic. Cover and set aside, as above.)

Knock the dough back with your fist and add the raisins, glacé cherries and flaked almonds. Gently knead until evenly incorporated.

Roll the dough out on a floured surface into a 30cm/12in long sausage. Carefully lift the dough onto a large baking sheet lined with non-stick baking parchment and shape it into a wreath, taking care to stick the ends together to join.

Cover the wreath with a tea towel and let it rise in a warm spot for about 30 minutes, or until the dough has visibly grown by at least half its size again. Heat the oven to 200°C/180°C fan/400°F.

Brush the top of the wreath with beaten egg and bake for about 25 minutes until rusty brown. Transfer to a wire rack to cool.

Once cool, mix the icing sugar, lemon juice and water together. Drizzle the glaze over the top and decorate with the cherries and almonds.

This is best served fresh the day it's baked.

Zwiebelzopf
Onion plait

MAKES ONE 30 × 17cm (12 × 7in) PLAIT

I wanted to include a savoury loaf in this book to be enjoyed for Abendbrot that encompasses true German flavour and Christmas spirit. Abendbrot, directly translated as 'evening bread', is the generic term for dinner in Germany, so called because traditionally the evening meal used to comprise simple slices of bread to be topped with cold meats, cheeses and fresh vegetables all laid out on the table. These days it isn't the case that the hot meal is eaten at lunchtime, as working practices and social views on this have changed. For my grandparents' generation, though, a hot meal at lunch was very much still practised and whenever I stayed with them in Bavaria, Abendbrot was a highlight – it felt liberating that everyone could pick and mix whatever they wanted to eat. I think it's a great blueprint for stress-free family suppers, and our evening meal is often guided by the principles of Abendbrot.

Caraway is used extensively in the German kitchen. I love it but also know that it can be divisive; simply leave it out if it's not your thing.

300g (2 cups plus 2 tbsp) strong white bread flour
150g (1⅓ cups) rye flour
1½ tsp fine sea salt
2 tsp sweet paprika
1 tsp caraway seeds
1 tbsp fresh thyme leaves

20g (¾oz) fresh yeast, or 10g (⅓oz) dried
180ml (¾ cup) tepid whole milk
200g (1 cup minus 1 tbsp) *Quark*
1 small onion, grated or blitzed in a food processor
1 egg, beaten

Put both flours, the salt, sweet paprika, caraway seeds and thyme into a large bowl and mix with a wooden spoon. Crumble the yeast (or sprinkle if using dried) into the tepid milk and stir to dissolve. Pour the yeasted milk into the flour mixture, add the *Quark* and onion and, using your hands, bring everything together into a rough dough. Tip out onto a floured surface and knead for about 10 minutes until elastic. Form it into a ball and nestle it into the bottom of the bowl. Cover with a tea towel and set aside in a warm spot to rise for about an hour, or until doubled in size. (Alternatively, put the flours, salt, sweet paprika,

caraway seeds and thyme into the bowl of a free-standing electric mixer fitted with a dough hook, pour in the yeasted milk, add the *Quark* and onion and knead for 5–8 minutes until elastic. Cover and set aside, as above.)

Once the dough has doubled in size, knock it back with your fist and line a large baking sheet with non-stick baking parchment.

Split the dough into three pieces. Sprinkle the work surface with water and, with wet hands, roll each piece into a sausage shape about 40cm/16in long. Place all three pieces of dough on the prepared baking sheet and braid them together, tucking the ends in and underneath. Cover the loaf with a tea towel and let it rise in a warm spot for 30 minutes, or until the dough has visibly grown by at least half its size again. Heat the oven to 210°C/190°C fan/410°F.

Brush the top of the loaf with beaten egg and bake for about 30 minutes until rusty brown. Transfer to a wire rack to cool.

This is best served still just warm the day it's baked, but if wrapped well will keep for 2 days.

Walnusskranz mit Camembert
Walnut and Camembert wreath

SERVES 4–6 WITH ADDITIONAL SIDES

This recipe is a bit of Abendbrot *fun. Every time I make it, the boys delight in it so much that it brings a smile to my lips just writing it down. I know it might seem overly gushing to say, but I really hope it's enjoyed with as much enthusiasm in your homes too.*

Baked or fried Camembert is a Bavarian speciality served with redcurrant sauce in most beer gardens and bars — while this isn't that, it's where the idea for the recipe came from. I like to serve mine with a crisp green salad and crudités alongside.

450g (3¼ cups) strong white bread flour, plus extra for dusting
1½ tsp fine sea salt
20g (¾oz) fresh yeast, or 10g (⅓oz) dried
200ml (¾ cup plus 1½ tbsp) tepid whole milk
200g (1 cup minus 1 tbsp) *Quark*
1 tbsp fresh thyme leaves, or ½ tbsp fresh rosemary, finely chopped

80g (3oz) walnuts, chopped
1 ripe Camembert in a wooden box

TO FINISH
1 egg, beaten
30g (1oz) walnuts, roughly chopped
3 tbsp extra virgin olive oil

Put the flour and salt into a large bowl and mix. Crumble the yeast (or sprinkle if using dried) into the tepid milk and stir to dissolve. Pour the yeasted milk into the flour and add the *Quark*. Using your hands, bring everything together into a rough dough. Tip the dough out onto a floured surface and knead for about 10 minutes until elastic. Form it into a ball and nestle it into the bottom of the bowl. Cover with a tea towel and set aside in a warm spot to rise for an hour, or until doubled in size. (Alternatively, put the flour and salt into the bowl of a free-standing electric mixer fitted with a dough hook, pour in the yeasted milk, add the *Quark*, and knead for 5–8 minutes until elastic. Cover and set aside, as above.)

Knock the dough back and add the herbs and walnuts. Gently knead to evenly incorporate.

Line a large baking sheet with non-stick baking parchment. Unwrap the Camembert, and place it back inside the box in the centre of the sheet.

Tip the dough out onto a floured surface. With floured hands, cut the dough in half and then cut each half into six equal pieces. Form each piece into a ball by tucking the sides into the bottom until you have a smooth-topped bun. Place six balls around the Camembert 1cm/⅜in away from the box and about 2cm/¾in apart. Now place the remaining balls in the spaces inside the first six balls, leaving 1cm/⅜in of room around each one.

Cover with a tea towel and let it rise in a warm spot for around 30 minutes, or until the dough has visibly grown by at least half its size again. Heat the oven to 200°C/180°C fan/400°F.

Brush the top of the buns with the beaten egg and sprinkle with chopped walnuts. Drizzle a tablespoon of olive oil onto the Camembert and bake for 20–25 minutes.

Once baked, slide the baking parchment (with the cheese and rolls on) off onto a large wooden board. Drizzle the Camembert and rolls with the remaining olive oil before tucking in while still hot.

171

Baiser

MERINGUES

There isn't a confection more fitting to Christmas than snowy meringues. Snowballs, snowmen, Christmas trees, wreaths, pavlovas, Santa hats, reindeer, candy canes, snowflakes, polar bears -- you name it and a meringue could be it. I had a lot of fun with this chapter, which I hope will translate over into your homes.

One of the best things about meringues is that they stay fresh for weeks, if not months on end, when stored in airtight containers. Another

good thing is that they can be transformed into an infinite number of desserts with the addition of a few simple ingredients: cream, custard, ice cream, yogurt, chestnuts, fresh fruit, frozen berries, chocolate, caramel -- the list goes on, all go well with meringues. I suppose what I'm saying is that although I've written the recipes in this chapter to be specific, they could just as well be made for any sweet dish you wish to turn them into.

Glückspilze
'Lucky' meringue mushrooms

MAKES ABOUT 20

Mushrooms are a huge part of German life, from family walks in the woods where they are foraged to the numerous regional dishes in which they are cooked – I think they're almost as 'German' and beloved as white asparagus is.

Mushrooms are seen as a symbol of good luck in Germany and they are often depicted in children's storybooks, Christmas cards, wrapping paper and tin boxes. They also come in the form of glass ornaments for the Christmas tree as well as edible marzipan confections (traditional at New Year), and in these light and crunchy 'mushroom' meringues. With a chewy centre, these meringue mushrooms are delectable on their own, but also make the most adorable 'lucky' decorations for a chocolate torte or a Yule log.

2 egg whites
140g (¾ cup plus 1 tsp) caster (superfine) sugar
80g (3oz) dark chocolate
¼ tsp coconut oil
1 tsp unsweetened cocoa powder

Heat the oven to 100°C/80°C fan/210°F and line two large baking sheets with non-stick baking parchment.

Put the egg whites into the bowl of a free-standing electric mixer fitted with a whisk attachment (or use a mixing bowl and a hand-held electric mixer), and whisk for a couple of minutes on a high speed until stiff peaks form. Reduce the speed and add the sugar one tablespoon at a time, whisking all the while, until fully incorporated and glossy.

To make the caps of the mushrooms, spoon 20 teaspoons of the mixture, spaced 2cm/¾in apart, onto one of the prepared baking sheets. Use the back of the spoon to flatten the mounds until they are between 2–3cm/¾–1¼in in diameter, then round off the tops.

To make the mushroom stalks, spoon heaped teaspoons of the mixture 2cm/¾in apart onto the second sheet. This time try to lift the

spoon up as you do so to create taller (around 3–4cm/1¼–1½in high) peaks.

Bake for 45 minutes. Don't open the oven door. Once the time is up, turn the oven off and let the meringues cool completely inside the oven.

Once the meringues are cooled, put the chocolate and coconut oil into a heatproof bowl set over a small saucepan with a 1cm/⅜in depth of water in the bottom. Heat on low then, once the chocolate starts melting, stir until glossy.

Spoon chocolate onto the underside of each mushroom cap. The chocolate will act as the glue to hold the stalk in place. While holding a cap in one hand, gently push a stalk into the centre of the chocolate-coated side – you will hear a cracking sound as it breaks through the base of the meringue cap; don't worry, it's a good thing as it means they will stick together well. Place cap-side down on the baking sheet and repeat with the remaining caps and stalks.

Once the chocolate has set (which will take an hour or so), turn them over onto their stalks (hopefully they will balance) and, using a sieve, dust the tops of the caps with cocoa powder.

Stored in an airtight container, these will keep well for about 2 weeks.

Baiserringe
Meringue wreaths for the tree

MAKES 12

These are lightly spiced with cinnamon and have the zest of an orange added to the mix, which goes so well with the scent of a pine tree. They are still delicious after a couple of weeks of hanging on the tree and make a brilliant dessert with whipped cream, custard and fruit (like a cross between a trifle and an Eton mess). We like it with bananas and raspberries, but strawberries, stewed apples, blueberries, leftover cranberry sauce even, would all be good.

2 egg whites
140g (¾ cup plus
  1 tsp) caster
  (superfine) sugar
½ tsp ground cinnamon

Finely grated zest of
  1 orange
Sprinkles and silver
  balls, to decorate
  (optional)

Heat the oven to 100°C/80°C fan/210°F and line a large baking sheet with non-stick baking parchment.

Put the egg whites into the bowl of a free-standing electric mixer fitted with a whisk attachment (or use a mixing bowl and a hand-held electric mixer) and whisk for a couple of minutes on a high speed until stiff peaks form. Turn the speed down and add the sugar one tablespoon at a time, whisking all the while, until it is all incorporated and you have a glossy meringue. Now add the cinnamon and orange zest and whisk for about 20 seconds until evenly mixed.

Spoon the meringue mixture into a piping bag fitted with a 1cm/⅜in star-shaped nozzle.

Pipe out wreaths of about 7cm/2¾in diameter. These are beautiful in all their snowy glory just as they are, but you can also choose, and we usually always do, to decorate them with sprinkles and/or silver balls.

Bake for 45 minutes. Don't open the oven door, but once the time is up turn the oven off and let the meringues cool completely inside the oven.

Once cooled they are ready to have ribbons threaded through and be hung on the tree.

Also pictured: Bunte Schokoladenkränze *(p.198),* Gewürzplätzchen *(p.194)*

Baisermäuse
Meringue mice

MAKES ABOUT 10

*As a child I would get a sugar mouse in my stocking each year.
I loved the idea of them but, charming as they seem, they're an edible
disappointment. Hard, bland and tooth-achingly sweet, they don't
have much going for them other than cute looks.*

*A meringue mouse, on the other hand, has bags of charm as well as flavour
and crunch. Too fragile for the bottom of a stocking, I make these each year
for Nikolaus and sit them alongside the boys' shoes on the stairs instead.*

2 egg whites
130g (¾ cup minus
  1 tsp) caster
  (superfine) sugar
1 tsp vanilla extract

TO DECORATE,
PER MOUSE
2 flaked (slivered)
  almonds (for ears)
2 raisins (for eyes)
1 whole hazelnut (for
  nose)
10cm/4in liquorice lace
  (for tail)

Heat the oven to 100°C/80°C fan/210°F and line a large baking sheet with non-stick baking parchment.

Put the egg whites into the bowl of a free-standing electric mixer fitted with a whisk attachment (or use a mixing bowl and a hand-held electric mixer) and whisk for a couple of minutes on a high speed until stiff peaks form. Turn the speed down and add the sugar one tablespoon at a time, whisking all the while, until it is all incorporated and you have a glossy meringue. Now add the vanilla extract and whisk for about 20 seconds until evenly mixed.

Spoon the meringue mixture into a piping bag fitted with a 2cm/¾in plain nozzle (or use a plastic freezer bag with a corner cut off to give a 2cm/¾in opening). Pipe the mixture into mouse shapes, wider at one end and tapering off towards the nose. They should be about 7cm/2¾in long. Although meringues don't spread, it's a good idea to leave 1cm/⅜in between each one.

Press the almonds gently into the position of the ears, followed by the raisins for eyes and the hazelnut for the nose.

Bake in the oven for 1–2 hours. After 1 hour the meringues will be crisp on the outside but soft and full of mallow within. After 1½ hours they will be chewy inside, and after 2 hours they will be crisp throughout. We actually like them at the mallow stage; it's up to you. Don't open the oven door, but once your desired time is up, turn the oven off and let the meringues cool completely inside the oven.

To add the tail, poke a small hole into the rear end of each mouse using a cake skewer and feed the liquorice lace into the hole, laying the longer part on the back of the mouse.

Stored in an airtight container, these will last for at least 3 weeks.

Baiserkranz mit heißen Himbeeren
Meringue wreath with hot raspberries

SERVES 6–8

This festive meringue dish is inspired by my favourite dessert of all time, Heiße Liebe, which directly translates as 'hot love' – as soon as you put the first spoonful into your mouth you'll understand why someone called it this. You might even end up dreaming about it; I do.

Heiße Liebe is popular in Austria and Alpine towns and, despite being served year round, I've always thought of it as a winter dessert. Like most good things, Heiße Liebe isn't complicated or pretending to be anything it's not. It's simply vanilla ice cream with hot vanilla-scented raspberries spooned over the top. Might not sound like much, but trust me when I say you want to try it. Hot, cold, sweet and tangy all in one spoonful, and as you get to the bottom of the dish you'll find a creamy soup of melted ice cream and raspberry juice that you'll start to eat increasingly slowly, anticipating the sadness you'll feel once it's gone. If you're not into Christmas pudding, this could be your answer to the perfect ending.

2 egg whites
120g (⅔ cup) caster
 (superfine) sugar
1 tsp vanilla extract
8 scoops of vanilla ice
 cream, to serve
Mint leaves, to decorate

FOR THE HOT
RASPBERRIES
800g (1lb 12oz) frozen
 raspberries
80g (½ cup minus
 1 tbsp) caster
 (superfine) sugar
1 tsp vanilla extract

ake the raspberries out of the freezer 3 hours before making the meringues and place them in a large saucepan to defrost. Add the sugar and vanilla extract and shake all of this together so that the sugar is dispersed through the raspberries.

Heat the oven to 100°C/80°C fan/210°F and line a large baking sheet with non-stick baking parchment.

Put the egg whites into the bowl of a free-standing electric mixer fitted with a whisk attachment (or use a mixing bowl and a hand-held electric mixer) and whisk for a couple of minutes on a high speed until stiff peaks form. Turn the speed down and add the sugar one tablespoon at a time, whisking all the while, until it is all incorporated and you have a glossy meringue. Now add the vanilla extract and whisk for about 20 seconds until evenly mixed.

Take tablespoons of the mixture and place them onto the prepared baking sheet to make 8 in total. Personally, I find roughly shaped meringues much more charming than perfectly round ones, but you can smooth them into ball shapes with the back of the spoon if you prefer.

Bake in the oven for 1½ hours. Don't open the over door, but once the time is up turn the oven off and let the meringues cool completely inside the oven. (The meringues will keep well for up to a month if stored in an airtight container and so can be made well in advance.)

Heat the raspberries gently until hot through, but not boiling. Try not to stir them at all as they will break up easily and it's nice to have some left whole (we're not making a coulis).

To assemble, arrange the meringues and balls of vanilla ice cream on a large platter, in a wreath shape. Pour over the hot raspberries, arrange some mint leaves decoratively on top and serve immediately.

Kaffee und Kuchen

COFFEE AND CAKE

Kaffee und Kuchen is a typical Sunday afternoon German ritual. Ok, it might not happen every Sunday of every month, just like we might not all roast a chicken with all the trimmings each week, but it is something that is practised with some form of regularity, unlike, say, an afternoon tea, which might happen once in a blue moon at home (I don't know many British people, me included, who take afternoon tea regularly).

Omi (my maternal grandmother) used to make her coffee so strong that you could 'stand a spoon in it', as she was often complemented on. And it's something I've come to realize wasn't just her quirk – dark, strong coffee is actually ingrained into German society, as much as it is in Italy and Scandinavian countries.

A typical *Kaffee und Kuchen* session has at least one, if not a couple of varieties of cake and a bowl of softly whipped vanilla-scented cream. But the best thing about it for me is the *Kaffeeklatsch*, which loosely translated means a gossip over a cup of coffee. The German word *gemütlich* describes this scene well, as does the Swedish *fika* or Danish *hygge*. Taking time to relax with friends over baked goods and several cups of coffee in a calm and inviting atmosphere (this is where the candles come in) surrounded by good smells and a sense of cosiness is what *Kaffee und Kuchen* is all about.

While a *Bunter Teller* is usually served to friends when they come over during Advent, I still think it's nice to have a seasonal cake on offer as well, making a total occasion of it.

Waffeln
Oat waffles

MAKES 8

In Germany waffles aren't a breakfast thing so much as an afternoon affair. They are usually eaten with lightly whipped vanilla-scented cream and are sprinkled with icing sugar alongside a coffee in place of a piece of cake. It's a tradition that I particularly enjoy on candlelit winter afternoons when the light dwindles around four o'clock.

I wrote this recipe for my friend Steffi, who meticulously veganizes almost every recipe she comes across. She really brought to my attention the art of writing flexible recipes for all dietary requirements. When I cook I often think of Steffi switching things up in her Berlin kitchen, and one day I hope we'll sit at the same table during Advent sharing a plate of these.

300ml (1¼ cups) milk (plant-based option for the vegan version)

120g (1 cup plus 1 tbsp) porridge oats

100g (1 cup minus 1 tbsp) rye or wholemeal (wholewheat) flour (buckwheat flour for a gluten-free option)

75g (⅓ cup) unsalted butter, melted, or 75ml (5 tbsp) sunflower or rapeseed oil

2 eggs, beaten (2 flax eggs for the vegan version)*

1½ tsp baking powder

½ tsp bicarbonate of soda (baking soda)

FOR THE VANILLA CREAM

300ml (1¼ cups) whipping cream (plant-based option for the vegan version)

2 tsp caster (superfine) sugar

½ tsp vanilla extract

* To make a flax egg mix 1 tbsp ground flax seeds with 3 tbsp water and set aside for 5 minutes before use.

Put the milk and oats into a big bowl, stir, then add the flour. Add the remaining ingredients and beat with a wooden spoon until everything is combined.

To make the vanilla cream, put the cream, sugar and vanilla extract into the bowl of a free-standing electric mixer fitted with a whisk attachment (or use a mixing bowl and a hand-held electric mixer) and whisk for a couple of minutes on a medium speed until soft peaks form. (Alternatively, whip by hand using a balloon whisk, although this will take a good few minutes longer.) Place to one side.

Heat and grease the waffle iron, then cook your waffles for about 2 minutes until golden brown.

Serve hot from the waffle iron with a dollop of vanilla cream.

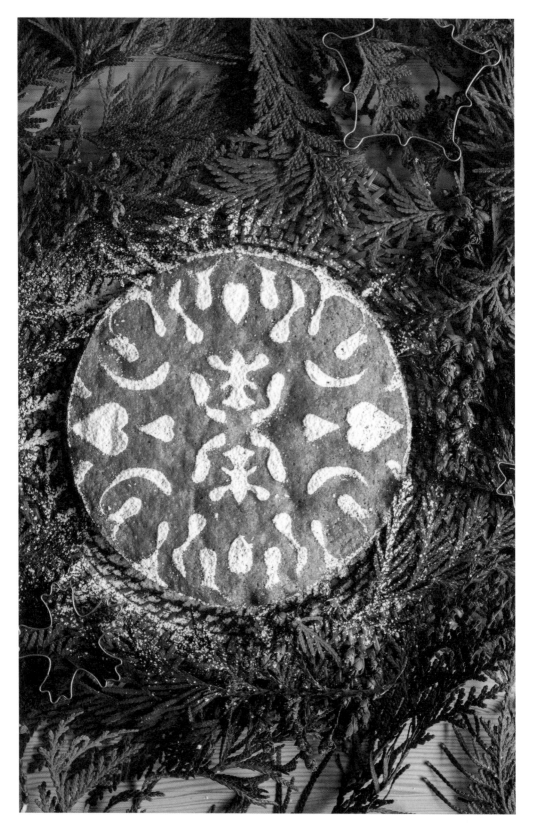

Schneeflocken-Marzipankuchen
Marzipan snowflake cake

SERVES 6

*This cake takes its inspiration from a Linzer biscuit. Two almondy
cake halves sandwiched together with a raspberry centre. Raspberry
jam has become the conserve of choice in a modern Linzer biscuit
but the Linzer tart (of which the biscuits are a descendant) was
originally filled with tart blackcurrant jam. To be honest, so long as
the jam has some punch to it I don't think it matters which one you
choose. I've used damson, sour cherry and redcurrant jelly as well as
the aforementioned, but strawberry and apricot would be too sweet.*

*Rather than ice this, I've played around with paper-cut snowflakes
as icing sugar templates and the results are beautifully festive;
a doily, too, works just as well.*

100g (¾ cup) unsalted
butter, at room temp

75g (⅓ cup plus 1 tbsp)
caster (superfine)
sugar

2 eggs, separated,
whites whisked to stiff
peaks

100g (3½oz) marzipan,
grated

75g (½ cup plus 1 tbsp)
plain (all-purpose)
flour

25g (3½ tbsp) ground
almonds (almond
flour)

1 tsp ground cinnamon

1 tsp baking powder

4 tbsp raspberry jam
(jelly)

Icing (confectioners')
sugar, for dusting

Heat the oven to 180°C/160°C fan/350°F and grease and line two 20cm/8in round cake tins (pans).

Put the butter and sugar into a large bowl and beat with a hand-held electric whisk until light and fluffy. Add the egg yolks and whisk again until combined. Add the grated marzipan, flour, ground almonds, cinnamon and baking powder, then stir until well mixed.

Fold the whisked egg whites into the batter, then divide the mixture evenly between the two cake tins and smooth the tops with a spatula.

Bake in the centre of the oven for about 20 minutes until golden brown and springy to the touch. Turn the cakes out onto a wire rack to cool.

Once cool, put one cake onto a plate, spoon the jam on top and spread it out evenly. Place the second cake on top.

Cut out a round piece of paper just larger than the cake. Fold it into four and cut an intricate snowflake design out of it. Unfold the piece of paper and lay it on top of the cake. Dust the top with icing sugar before carefully removing the paper. You should be left with a beautiful delicate snowflake on top of your cake.

Stored in an airtight container, this cake will keep well for up to 3 days.

Weihnachtsgugelhupf
Christmas Gugelhupf

MAKES 1 (SERVES 8)

A classic, enriched, yeasted dough cake – think of it like the German version of a fruit loaf, just as good sliced and eaten fresh as it is toasted for breakfast.

50g (1¾oz) raisins
50g (1¾oz) currants
50g (1¾oz) mixed peel
1 tbsp dark rum or
　brandy
75ml (5 tbsp) tepid milk
20g (¾oz) fresh yeast,
　or 10g (⅓oz) dried
250g (1¾ cups plus
　2 tbsp) plain
　(all-purpose) flour
½ tsp fine sea salt
80g (½ cup minus 2
　tsp) caster (superfine)
　sugar
150g (⅔ cup) unsalted
　butter, at room temp,
　plus extra for greasing

2 eggs
1½ tsp vanilla extract
Finely grated zest of
　½ lemon
Finely grated zest of
　½ orange
50g (1¾oz) flaked
　(slivered) almonds
1 tbsp fine semolina
Icing (confectioners')
　sugar, for dusting

You will need a small,
　20cm/8in *Gugelhupf*
　tin.

Put all the dried fruit into a small bowl, pour over the rum and set aside to steep.

Put the milk into a small jug or bowl, crumble in the yeast (or sprinkle if using dried) and stir to dissolve. If using a free-standing electric mixer, put the flour, salt, sugar, butter, eggs and vanilla extract into the bowl and pour over the yeasted milk. Using the paddle attachment, mix for a couple of minutes until a sticky, dense dough is formed – it will be more like the consistency of a cake batter than bread. Cover the bowl with a tea towel and set aside in a warm place to rise for about an hour until the dough has expanded a little.

If making the dough by hand, dissolve the yeast in the milk as above. Put the flour and salt into a large mixing bowl. In a separate bowl, beat the sugar and butter together until creamy. Add the eggs and beat again; don't worry if the mixture looks split at this stage. Add the yeasted milk, butter mixture and vanilla extract to the flour. Either using your hands or a wooden spoon, mix everything together until a sticky, dense dough is formed. Cover and set aside to rise.

Add the rum-soaked fruit, citrus zests and flaked almonds to the dough and mix through.

Butter the insides of the *Gugelphupf* tin and sprinkle with the semolina, shaking it around so it coats the entire surface (this acts as a non-stick lining). Spoon the dough into the tin, cover with a tea towel and place in a warm spot for 30–45 minutes to rise for a second time.

Heat the oven to 200°C/180°C fan/400°F.

Bake for 45–55 minutes until the crust is deep brown and a metal skewer comes out clean when inserted into the deepest part of the cake. Check after 30 minutes, as it may need to be covered with foil to prevent it from browning too much on top.

Let cool in the tin for 20 minutes before turning the cake out onto a wire rack – this is really important as it won't come out clean otherwise. Dust with icing (confectioners') sugar.

This will keep for 3 days stored in an airtight container.

Gewürzter Schokoladenkuchen
Spiced chocolate and prune fudge cake

MAKES 1 (SERVES 8)

This moist, dense cake is made with buckwheat flour, making it gluten free. It's so rich and indulgent it can also double as dessert.

100g (3½oz) prunes, pitted
100ml (7 tbsp) just-boiled water
200g (¾ cup plus 2 tbsp) unsalted butter, at room temp, plus extra for greasing
225g (1 cup plus 2 tbsp) dark brown sugar
2 eggs
1 tsp vanilla extract
100g (3½oz) dark chocolate (70% cocoa solids), melted
100g (3½oz) buckwheat flour
50g (1¾oz) unsweetened cocoa powder

1½ tsp ground cinnamon
½ tsp ground cardamom
50g (⅓ cup) cornflour (cornstarch)
1 tsp baking powder (ensure gluten-free, if necessary)
1 tsp bicarbonate of soda (baking soda)

FOR THE FROSTING
225g (8oz) dark chocolate (50% cocoa solids), broken into pieces
300ml (1¼ cups) double (heavy) cream

TO DECORATE
Sprig of holly, orange slices or bay leaves

 ut the prunes into a small bowl and pour the just-boiled water over them. Leave to soak and soften for 30 minutes.

Heat the oven to 180°C/160°C fan/350°F. Grease and line a 23cm/9in springform cake tin (pan).

Put the butter, sugar and soaked prunes (including liquid) into a food processor and blitz until smooth. Add the eggs and vanilla extract and blitz until evenly combined – it may look split at this stage, but this is normal. Pour the melted chocolate into the mixture and blitz once more until mixed through.

Now add the remaining ingredients and blitz for about 30 seconds until the batter is smooth. Tip the batter into the prepared tin and smooth the top with a spatula.

Bake in the centre of the oven for 30 minutes, or until set on top and just starting to brown. A metal skewer inserted into the centre of the cake won't, and should not, come out clean – the middle of this cake is fudgy, hence its name, and because of this it will sink in the centre as it cools.

Cool in the tin, turn out onto a wire rack, then turn the correct way up onto a serving plate.

To make the frosting, put the chocolate into a large mixing bowl. Heat the cream in a saucepan over a medium-high heat, stirring from time to time, until it just comes to the boil. Take off the heat and pour immediately onto the chocolate. Using a wooden spoon, beat the chocolate and cream together until smooth and glossy; the heat from the cream will melt the chocolate.

Spoon the frosting generously into the dip in the centre of the cake. Decorate with a sprig of holly, some dried orange slices, bay leaves – whatever takes your fancy really.

Alternatively, if you choose not to frost this, it is good eaten warm (but not hot straight out of the oven) for dessert with a dollop of crème fraîche on the side, possibly some hot raspberries (see page 180) too.

Unfrosted, it will keep well in an airtight tin for 3 days.

Baumschmuck

TREE DECORATIONS

I don't think there are many better smells in the world than those that come along with Advent. From the spiced biscuits baking in the oven, to those that hang on the tree, and the haze of just-blown-out candles lingering in the air, to the cold that clings to your clothes and hair as you enter a warm house... the *Glühwein* simmering away on the stovetop, to the spritz of essential oil released from a clementine as it's being peeled, and the heady fragrance of rum-soaked fruit, to the resinous scent of pine from the tree — Advent throws its arms around you with its warm, welcoming scent. This chapter is as much about these magical smells as it is about flavour.

Homemade tree decorations encompass all that I love about Christmas. While I'm a fan of shiny glass baubles and the odd kitsch ornament too, it's tree biscuits, dried orange slices and apple rings that really tug at my heart strings, for they hold an almost childlike innocence. Unlike glass or plastic knick-knacks, these dangling edible treats are transient objects, made all the more special because one minute they're here and the next they're gobbled up.

Gewürzplätzchen
Spiced biscuits to hang on the tree

*These are your stereotypical spiced tree biscuits that will stay
looking pretty for an incredibly long time. I have a friend who
has used the same biscuits to hang on her tree several years running.
How she managed to resist eating them I have no idea, because
these biscuits don't stand a hope of surviving beyond the first week
of Advent in our house, which is why we usually bake a double batch
and reserve half to hang in the middle of December once the
tree decoration annihilation has begun in earnest.*

150g (⅔ cup) unsalted
butter
225g (1 cup plus
2 tbsp) soft light
brown sugar
6 tbsp golden syrup
3 tbsp *Rübenkraut*
(sugar beet syrup, see
page 13) or treacle
2 tsp bicarbonate of
soda (baking soda)
2 tbsp just-boiled water
500g (3¾ cups) plain
(all-purpose) flour

2 tsp ground ginger
2 tsp ground cinnamon
1 tsp ground cloves
½ tsp grated nutmeg
Pinch of fine sea salt

FOR THE ICING
2 egg whites
425g (3 cups) icing
(confectioners') sugar,
sifted
Spritz of lemon juice

Heat the oven to 200°C/180°C fan/400°F
and line two or three baking sheets
with non-stick baking parchment.

Melt the butter, sugar, golden syrup
and *Rübenkraut* in a saucepan over a medium
heat, stirring from time to time, until everything
is viscous.

In a small mug, dissolve the bicarbonate of soda
in the just-boiled water.

Put all of the dry ingredients into a large
mixing bowl, pour over the buttery sugar
and the dissolved bicarbonate of soda. Mix
everything together with a wooden spoon
until a dense dough is formed.

Divide the dough into three parts to make
it easier to work with. Roll out each part
separately to around 3mm/⅛in thick (this
dough doesn't really stick so there is no need
to flour the work surface). Cut out shapes using
various festive cookie cutters (see pages 258–9)
and place on the prepared baking sheets.
Re-roll all the dough offcuts into more biscuits.

Bake in the oven for about 8 minutes until
just starting to brown. Take out of the oven and,
using a wooden skewer, immediately make a
hole near the top of each biscuit. Transfer to a
wire rack and leave to cool before decorating.

While the biscuits are cooling, make the icing
by beating all the ingredients together in a
large bowl, using a wooden spoon, until glossy
and smooth. Spoon the icing into a piping bag
fitted with a fine nozzle and decorate away.
Once the icing has set thread the holes with
string, ready to hang on the tree.

These will keep well for 2 months stored in
an airtight container, and are still perfectly
edible after 3 weeks on the Christmas tree.

Apfelringe
Dried apple rings

MAKES ABOUT 24

Aside from storing apples in newspaper to last the winter or making apple sauce to freeze and bottle, these dried rings are the best and easiest way of preserving this fruit. They have a sherbet tang to them and a pleasant chewy texture.

My great-grandmother used to string her apple rings up to dry out above the wood-burning stoves in her kitchen and living room, which always struck me as an ingenious way to decorate as well as preserve.

You can, of course, make these without a wood-burning stove or fireplace to hang them above, and below are the instructions for using an oven. I sometimes also dry ours out on wire racks balanced on the radiators, and the residual oven heat from baking works really well too.

Juice of 1 lemon
⅛ tsp fine sea salt
3 eating apples

eat the oven to 70°C/50°C fan/160°F. Stir the lemon juice and salt together in a small bowl until the salt has completely dissolved.

Slice the apples into 2mm/¹⁄₁₆in thick rounds, keeping the skin and core intact – the latter has a lovely star shape in the centre where the pips sit. I find using a mandoline helps to slice the apples thinly enough.

Dip each apple ring into the lemon mixture to coat all over. Lay on wire racks and place them in the oven to dry out for about 45 minutes–

1 hour. You're aiming for the same texture as a chamois leather.

Alternatively, balance the wire racks on the top of a radiator, or place in an airing cupboard, to dry for 48 hours, turning each slice over after 24 hours.

If you wish to hang these on the tree, thread a needle with some fine cotton and feed it through the apple near the skin. Tie the cotton into a loop and it's now ready to hang.

These will keep for a couple of months if stored in an airtight container, but will be fine and still edible after 3 weeks of hanging on the tree.

Also pictured: Gewürzplätzchen *(p.194),* Orangenscheiben *(p.199)*

Bunte Schokoladenkränze
Chocolate sprinkle wreaths

MAKES ABOUT 20

I grew up with these dangling from our Christmas tree at home.
Much as I loved them, I always secretly envied the foil-wrapped
chocolate baubles and Santas on other people's trees too. Still,
I don't seem to be able to break from tradition and there's no
sight of foiled tree chocolates in my house as an adult either.

200g (7oz) dark
  chocolate (50%
  cocoa solids),
  broken into pieces

¼ tsp coconut oil
Hundreds and
  thousands or
  colourful sprinkles

ut the chocolate and coconut oil into a heatproof bowl. Place the bowl over a small saucepan with a 1cm/⅜in depth of water in the bottom. Turn the heat on low and wait for the chocolate to melt. Once the chocolate starts melting, stir it so that the coconut oil is evenly dispersed. Take it off the heat once the chocolate is fluid and glossy.

Line two baking sheets with non-stick baking parchment. Use a tablespoon to scoop some of the chocolate out of the bowl and carefully tilt the spoon to dribble the chocolate onto the baking parchment in a circular motion. It doesn't really matter how big you make these, but I usually make them with a diameter of 6–7cm/2½–2¾in. Repeat until all the chocolate is used up.

Now sprinkle each chocolate wreath generously with hundreds and thousands (my preference and the more traditional choice) or sprinkles. Let them set solid on the sheets; this can take anything up to three hours.

It's a good idea to have cold hands when you're ready to string these up to avoid the chocolate melting. Cut pieces of string around 15–18cm/6–7in long, loop the string through each decoration and tie it at the top; they are now ready to hang on the tree.

Stored in an airtight container, these will last for up to a month. And if you haven't eaten them all before it's time to take the tree down, you can melt them using the same method as above, and pour the warm sprinkle chocolate sauce over ice cream.

Pictured on page 176

Orangenscheiben
Dried orange slices

MAKES ABOUT 36

It's hard to think of Christmas without the mention of oranges or satsumas. For many of us around the world they are an integral part of festivities. Traditionally found in German children's boots and shoes on the morning of 6ᵗʰ December, or as part of a Bunter Teller on the 24ᵗʰ December, satsumas (or oranges) are a welcome burst of vitamins and freshness amidst all the sugary biscuits and sweet treats.

More of a process than a recipe, the smell of these orange slices drying in the oven drives me almost wild. These take a while to dry out, so it's good to set a morning aside for them, and an ideal time to write Christmas cards or wrap presents at the kitchen table, engulfed in their perfume.

These are just as pretty on the tree as they are dangling in a window, like intricate panes of stained glass. I also like to use them as cake toppers or slipped into a festive cocktail as a garnish.

3 oranges or satsumas

Heat the oven to 90°C/70°C fan/195°F and line two large baking sheets with non-stick baking parchment.

Slice the oranges into 2mm/¹⁄₁₆in thick rounds. I find using a mandoline helps to slice them thinly enough.

Lay the orange slices out on both sheets and bake in the oven for 2–4 hours, turning each slice every hour to ensure it dries out evenly. I tend to like mine after 2 hours so they're still a vibrant orange and retain much of their citrus scent. If you like them darker, dry them out for longer.

These look pretty in a bowl with star anise on the table and are by far the best (and dare I say only) pot pourri that should be allowed in the house.

If you wish to hang these on the tree or in the window, thread a needle with some fine cotton and feed it through the orange near the skin. Tie the cotton into a loop and it's now ready to hang.

Stored in an airtight container these will last indefinitely. If you don't intend to eat them, there is no need to keep them airtight.

Pictured on page 196

Butterplätzchen

BUTTER BISCUITS

Butter biscuits are the backbone of any *Bunter Teller*. Often glazed with icing and sprinkles, they're usually the first biscuits children learn to make at Advent, which is why, as adults, we still have such a strong connection with them.

The varieties of butter biscuits (or sugar biscuits if you prefer) are endless. If you find a good basic recipe (*Adventsröschen* or orange biscuits are a good place to start) you can dress them up or down as you please. Adding a flavouring or two changes the biscuits completely; citrus

zest, candied peel, dried fruit, spices and natural extracts such as vanilla, coffee and almond all make for good options.

Aside from the *Vanillekipferl*, which I only make at Christmas time, I would say the rest are all-year-round recipes, despite being most popular during Advent.

I hope you have fun with this chapter tailoring the biscuits to your individual tastes and thereby creating new traditions in your homes.

Vanillekipferl
Vanilla crescents

MAKES ABOUT 50

Vanillekipferl *originate from Vienna in Austria but versions of them are loved and baked throughout Germany, Poland, Hungary and Switzerland too. They are a non-negotiable must during Advent for me and I regularly eat one with the first coffee of the day while it's still pitch black outside – there's something most satisfying about eating a moon-shaped biscuit while the moon is still visible in the sky.*

This recipe is for the classic Austrian version made with ground almonds, which I find creamy and sweet, but ground hazelnuts are delicious too and in Hungary walnut varieties are the most popular.

Vanillekipferl are renowned for their light, crumbly texture and thick icing sugar coat, which clings to each biscuit, giving them their signature flavour. The icing sugar is sifted on in heavy drifts as soon as the biscuits are out of the oven, so the under layer almost melts into the biscuit, while the outer layer stays fluffy and light. These are one of those foods you cannot eat or even think about without licking your lips.

180g (1⅓ cups) plain (all-purpose) flour
80g (⅔ cup) ground almonds (almond flour)
Pinch of fine sea salt
125g (½ cup plus 1 tbsp) unsalted butter, at room temp

75g (½ cup) icing (confectioners') sugar, plus plenty of extra to dust
1 tsp vanilla extract
1 egg yolk

ombine the flour, ground almonds and salt together in a mixing bowl. Add the butter and gently work it into the dry ingredients with your fingertips until it resembles something similar to breadcrumbs. Now add the icing sugar and mix through so it's evenly dispersed. Add the vanilla extract along with the egg yolk and bring the dough together with your hands. Knead for about 3 minutes until a soft, pliable dough is formed. (Alternatively, put all the ingredients into the bowl of an electric mixer fitted with the paddle attachment and beat to a pliable dough on a low speed for a couple of minutes.)

Cover and refrigerate the dough for 1 hour.

Heat the oven to 180°C/160°C fan/350°F and line two large baking sheets with non-stick baking parchment.

Take small teaspoon-sized pieces of dough and roll them into little sausages, 5cm/2in long, with tapered edges, then form each into a crescent shape and place gently on a baking sheet.

Bake for about 12 minutes until just starting to colour. Leave to cool on the sheet for a minute, then transfer to a wire rack. While the biscuits are still hot, liberally sift over icing sugar to dust.

Once completely cool, store the biscuits in an airtight container. They will last a good 3 weeks.

Heidesand
Sandy shortbread

MAKES 30

Heidesand are Germany's equivalent to shortbread. The biscuits are inspired by the Lüneburger Heide (Lüneburg Heath) in Northern Germany. This area between the cities of Hamburg, Bremen and Hannover boasts particularly sandy soil (deposited from glaciers) and the landscape is famously covered in a purple carpet of heather during August and September. The buttery dough is supposed to replicate the sandy earth of the region. Despite having their roots in Lower Saxony, these biscuits are loved across the whole country and are baked in countless households up and down the land during the Advent period.

200g (1½ cups) plain (all-purpose) flour
75g (⅔ cup) ground almonds (almond flour)
Pinch of fine sea salt
150g (⅔ cup) unsalted butter, at room temp

75g (½ cup) icing (confectioners') sugar
1 tsp vanilla extract
3–4 tbsp caster (superfine) sugar

Heat the oven to 180°C/160°C fan/350°F and line two large baking sheets with non-stick baking parchment.

Put the flour, ground almonds and salt into a large mixing bowl. Add the butter and gently work it into the dry ingredients with your fingertips until it resembles something similar to breadcrumbs. Now add the icing sugar and mix through so it's evenly dispersed. Spoon in the vanilla extract and bring the dough together with your hands. Knead for about 3 minutes until a soft, pliable dough is formed.

(Alternatively, put all the ingredients into the bowl of an electric mixer fitted with the paddle attachment and beat to a pliable dough on a low speed for a couple of minutes.)

Pinch off walnut-sized pieces of dough and roll them into balls between the palms of your hands. As you lay each piece of dough onto a baking sheet, flatten it slightly with the underside of your fingers to form a round about 1cm/⅜in thick.

Bake in the oven for 12–15 minutes until just golden.

Put the caster sugar into a dish and roll each biscuit in it while still hot, straight from the oven, ensuring that all sides are covered. Place the biscuits on a wire rack to cool completely.

Stored in an airtight tin, they should keep well for 10 days to 2 weeks.

Orangenplätzchen
Iced orange biscuits

MAKES ABOUT 24

I make these biscuits as animal cut-outs with our youngest son, Aidan, throughout the year — we're particularly fond of them as part of the birthday tea table. At Christmas time we put the animals away and bring out the stars, bells and angels instead.

Making these with Aidan is filed into the long-term memory bank of my mind and I know it's a moment I will travel back to often in the future once he has long left home. I don't care how much of a cliché it is to admit this; I truly believe baking with your children can soften the universal parental pain of time flying by too fast. If you can relate to this, try making these with your little one.

100g (¾ cup) plain (all-purpose) flour
Pinch of fine sea salt
60g (5 tbsp) unsalted butter, at room temp
Finely grated zest of ½ orange or 1 clementine
40g (2½ tbsp) caster (superfine) sugar
2 egg yolks

FOR THE ICING
100g (scant ¾ cup) icing (confectioners') sugar, sifted, plus extra for dusting
1 tbsp plus 1 tsp orange juice
Finely grated zest of ½ orange

TO DECORATE
Sprinkles, silver balls, small jelly sweets (candies)

Heat the oven to 180°C/160°C fan/350°F and line a large baking sheet (or two) with non-stick baking parchment.

Put the flour and salt into a large mixing bowl (I say large because if small hands are involved things tend to fly everywhere, though the actual quantities for this recipe are quite small). Add the butter along with the orange zest and gently work it into the dry ingredients with your fingertips until it resembles something similar to breadcrumbs.

Now add the sugar and mix through so it's evenly dispersed. Add the egg yolks and bring the dough together with your hands. Knead for about 3 minutes until a soft, pliable dough is formed.

If using a free-standing electric mixer (I never do for such small quantities or if I'm baking with children, but there's nothing to stop you doing it, especially if short on time) put all the ingredients into the mixer bowl and use the paddle attachment to beat everything together to a pliable dough on a low speed for a couple of minutes.

Dust the work surface with icing sugar and roll the dough out to a thickness of about 3mm/⅛in. Choose any cookie cutters you wish to cut out shapes with (see pages 258–9), re-rolling the dough offcuts into more biscuits. Place on a prepared baking sheet, leaving 1cm/⅜in between each one. Bake in the oven for 12–15 minutes until just golden but not brown. Carefully transfer the biscuits on to a wire rack to cool completely.

Continued overleaf

While the biscuits are cooling, make the icing by mixing all the ingredients together in a small bowl until smooth and glossy.

Decorate each biscuit first with icing – we like to spread the icing to cover the top but you can drizzle it too if you wish. Finally, sprinkle away with your choice of topping.

Let the icing set (this should take about 1–2 hours) before storing in an airtight container where they should keep well for about 2 weeks. The biscuits will start off crunchy but will soften over time.

VARIATIONS

As I mentioned in the introduction to this chapter, the variations for this recipe are pretty endless. Here are two of my favourite alternatives:

Caraway and lemon

Add ¼ teaspoon of caraway seeds to the dough and switch the orange zest for lemon. Likewise, make the icing with lemon zest and juice instead of orange.

Clove and honey

Add ¼ teaspoon of ground cloves to the dough and switch the orange zest for lemon. Make the icing with 1 tablespoon of lemon juice and 1 teaspoon of honey.

Adventsröschen
Advent cut-outs

MAKES ABOUT 55

These buttery biscuits are very short; by that I mean at first crunchy, then crumbly and of a melt-in-your mouth texture. They are brushed with egg yolk, which gives them a deep golden lustre. Thinking about their flavour, probably the most similar biscuits you could compare them to are French sablé biscuits.

As I mentioned in the introduction, these can be jazzed up with other flavourings; the finely grated zest of 1 orange is lovely in these, as is ½ teaspoon of ground cinnamon.

200g (1½ cups) plain (all-purpose) flour
50g (3½ tbsp) cornflour (cornstarch)
Pinch of fine sea salt
120g (½ cup plus 1 tsp) unsalted butter, at room temp

100g (½ cup plus ½ tbsp) caster (superfine) sugar
1 tsp vanilla extract
2 tbsp whole milk
Icing (confectioners') sugar, for dusting
1 egg yolk

Heat the oven to 180°C/160°C fan/350°F and line two large baking sheets with non-stick baking parchment.

Combine the flours and salt together in a mixing bowl. Add the butter and gently work it into the dry ingredients with your fingertips until it resembles something similar to breadcrumbs. Now add the caster sugar and mix through so it's evenly dispersed. Add the vanilla extract along with the milk and bring the dough together with your hands. Knead for about 3 minutes until a soft, pliable dough is formed. (Alternatively, put all the ingredients except the icing sugar and egg yolk into the bowl of a free-standing electric mixer fitted with the paddle attachment and beat to a pliable dough on a low speed for a couple of minutes.)

Dust the work surface with icing sugar and roll the dough out to a thickness of 3mm/⅛in. Cut out biscuits with a fluted cutter (see pages 258–9) and place on the prepared baking sheets, leaving a 1cm/⅜in gap between them. Re-roll the dough offcuts into more biscuits.

Gently brush the top of all the biscuits with the egg yolk and bake in the oven for 12–15 minutes until golden brown.

Leave to cool on the sheets for a minute, then transfer to a wire rack to cool completely. Stored in an airtight tin, these will keep well for 2 weeks.

Kaffeeplätzchen
Coffee fondant biscuits

MAKES ABOUT 22

*I am the only coffee appreciator in our household. As well as drinking several cups
a day I also love anything remotely coffee-flavoured, such as éclairs and coffee
creams (usually the last lonely chocolate in the box, except for when I'm around).*

*When it comes to food and the enjoyment brought about through eating, I like
to please everyone in this house. While I might be the cook, and therefore have the
ultimate say in what ends up on everyone's plates, it's very rare that I'll feed the
people I love things they openly dislike.*

*So, I wrote this recipe for myself – a true indulgence, and every time I eat one I feel it.
I hope these buttery biscuits make some of you out there as happy as they make me.*

50g (1¾oz) hazelnuts,
   toasted and finely
   ground
12g (1½ tbsp) cornflour
   (cornstarch)
150g (¾ cup) plain
   (all-purpose) flour
Pinch of fine sea salt
125g (½ cup plus
   1 tbsp) unsalted
   butter, at room temp
90g (½ cup minus
   ½ tbsp) dark brown
   sugar
1 tbsp strong coffee
   (espresso strong)

FOR THE ICING
2 tbsp unsalted butter
2 tbsp strong coffee
200g (scant 1½ cups)
   icing (confectioners')
   sugar, sifted, plus
   extra for dusting

TO DECORATE
Whole hazelnuts or
   chocolate coffee
   beans

Heat the oven to 200°C/180°C fan/400°F
and line two large baking sheets with
non-stick baking parchment.

Combine the ground hazelnuts, flours
and salt together in a bowl. Add the butter
and rub it into the dry ingredients with your
fingertips until it resembles fine breadcrumbs.
Now add the sugar and mix to evenly disperse.
Add the coffee and bring the dough together
with your hands. Knead for about 3 minutes
until soft and pliable. (Alternatively, put all the
ingredients into the bowl of a free-standing
electric mixer fitted with the paddle attachment
and beat to a pliable dough on a low speed for
a couple of minutes.)

Dust the work surface with icing sugar and
roll the dough out to a thickness of 3mm/⅛in.
Cut out the biscuits using a round, fluted
cookie cutter (see pages 258–9), and place on
the prepared baking sheets, leaving 2cm/¾in
between each one. Re-roll all the dough offcuts
into more biscuits.

Bake in the oven for 8–10 minutes until just
slightly browned. Allow to cool on the sheets
for a minute or two before transferring over
to a wire rack to cool completely.

Once the biscuits have cooled, make the icing
by melting the butter into the coffee in a
saucepan over a low heat. Once melted, whisk in
the icing sugar until smooth and glossy. Working
quickly, as the top layer of icing sets quite fast,
ice the top of each biscuit. Place a hazelnut or
a chocolate coffee bean in the centre of each.

Leave the biscuits for an hour or two until the
icing has completely set.

Stored in an airtight container these will keep
for up to two weeks (possibly more, but I'm yet
to find that out).

20

Hexenhaus

GINGERBREAD HOUSE

Depicted in the mouth-watering Grimm Brothers' fairy tale *Hänsel und Gretel*, gingerbread houses conjure up images of deep, dark woods full of mystery, and it's where their German name, *Hexenhaus* (witch's house) is derived from. Made out of *Lebkuchen*, one of the oldest festive German biscuits, it's little wonder that they have now become synonymous with Christmas time too.

I don't want to shatter any fairy-tale illusions here, but I want you to know that we never manage to achieve a picture book perfect house at home. While I love to wander through stall after stall of perfectly piped icicle-hung houses at the *Weihnachtsmarkt*, and think they make some of the most magical Christmas shop window displays, the homemade reality is somewhat different.

My boys see the annual festive task of building the *Hexenhaus* as an opportunity to cram as many jelly sweets and chocolates as they can onto the house and into their mouths while I'm not looking — I don't resist, it's part and parcel of festivities.

Hexenhaus
Gingerbread house

MAKES 1

Gingerbread houses look just as pretty, if not more so, decorated with dried
or candied fruit and nuts as they do with jellied sweets and chocolate.

750g (5¾ cups) plain (all-purpose) flour
3 tsp ground ginger
3 tsp ground cinnamon
1 tsp ground cloves
¾ tsp fine sea salt
225g (1 cup) unsalted butter
375g (2 cups minus 2 tbsp) soft light brown sugar
12 tbsp golden syrup
3 tsp bicarbonate of soda (baking soda)
3 tbsp just-boiled water

FOR THE ICING
450g (3¼ cups) icing (confectioners') sugar, sifted
2 large egg whites

TO DECORATE
Sweets (candies) such as Smarties, Jelly Tots, liquorice or dried/candied fruit and nuts

 eat the oven to 200°C/180°C fan/400°F.

Put the flour, spices and salt into a large mixing bowl. Stir with a wooden spoon until all the ingredients are evenly mixed. Melt the butter, brown sugar and golden syrup in a saucepan over a low heat, stirring until evenly combined. Pour the butter mixture over the flour mixture. Mix the bicarb and just-boiled water together in a little bowl and pour this over the other ingredients.

Use a wooden spoon to mix everything into a stiff dough, then knead with your hands for a minute or two until silky. Divide into three equal pieces.

Lay a large baking sheet-sized piece of non-stick baking parchment on the work surface. Roll one piece of dough out to a 5mm/⅛in thickness and the size of an A4 sheet of paper. Trim the edges to neaten. Slide the parchment onto a baking sheet. This is the base of the house.

Do the same again but this time cut the A4-sized piece of dough in half, so that you now have two A5-sized pieces of dough. If possible, spread the two pieces apart a little to avoid sticking. Slide the parchment onto a baking sheet. These pieces are the roof.

Place the sheets into the oven and bake for 10–14 minutes until deep golden brown all over. Remove from the oven, allow to cool and stiffen slightly on the sheets for a few minutes before transferring to a wire rack to cool completely.

Continued overleaf

While the first lot of dough is baking, roll out the third piece of dough just as in the last step. This time trim 3cm/1¼in from the top of the shorter side of each A5 piece. Now measure halfway in (this should be 7.5cm/3in from each side) and cut long-sided triangles from the base to this point. Slide the parchment onto a baking sheet. These are both gable ends of the house.

Knead all the dough offcuts together and roll out on a piece of baking parchment until 5mm/⅛in thick. Cut out Christmas tree shapes and a couple of small triangles to hold the Christmas trees upright. Any spare dough can be used for Christmas tree decorations (see note opposite).

Bake the last two sheets in the oven the same as before but check the sheet with the trees and decorations after 8 minutes as these pieces will cook faster. Transfer to a wire rack to cool.

As soon as the triangle sides of the house are baked, cut out a little mouse hole shape for the door at the base of one of them. A star shaped window cut out with a cookie cutter also looks pretty just below the top of the triangle. Transfer the triangles to a wire rack to cool. (Alternatively, leave to cool and then simply pipe on a door and window with icing, as pictured.)

Using a wooden spoon, beat the icing sugar and egg whites together in a bowl until a thick icing forms.

Place the A4 gingerbread base on a large wooden board. Pipe or spread a 5mm/⅛in thick ribbon of icing along one of the shorter edges of each roof piece and all the way around the triangular sides.

Now, using a couple of pairs of hands, assemble the house. Start by holding the triangular house ends vertically and resting the roof pieces on the diagonal edges. (I like to have a 1cm/⅜in roof overhang on the front and back of the house.) Pipe some more icing onto the top edge of the roof to ensure it sticks together properly.

Pipe or spoon a small amount of icing onto the back of each sweet and decorate your gingerbread house with wild abandon.

Dollop some icing onto the base wherever you wish to plant a tree and carefully balance the tree in place, using the triangular support.

The house will be edible for a couple of weeks, but is best eaten within the first 5 days. To turn stale gingerbread into a Christmas trifle: soak gingerbread in a mixture of brandy and apple juice, top with blackberry and apple compote, followed by custard, then softly whipped cream and lastly a sprinkling of toasted flaked almonds.

NOTE

I also use this dough recipe for tree decorations or simple iced biscuits. Roll out to a 5mm/⅛in thickness and cut the dough into desired shapes with cookie cutters. Bake for 8–10 minutes. Take out of the oven and, using a wooden skewer, immediately make a hole near the top of the decoration, transfer to a wire rack and leave to cool before decorating and adding string.

Weihnachtskonfekt

CHRISTMAS CONFECTIONS

As well as adding a different dimension to a *Bunter Teller*, all of these make lovely boxed gifts.

Each year I spend hours making and then boxing up various confections for different family members and friends – the best part, of course, is the giving. The idea of handing over something homemade during a time of year where commercialism seems to have overtaken festive spirit restores the balance somewhat.

To sometimes find myself on the receiving end of such gifts too brings a tear to my eye. For the past few years my friend Sophie has posted us an exquisitely packaged box full of creamy homemade fudge at the start of December. While I don't ever expect it, I would be lying if I said I didn't long for it.

I hope that as well as enjoying these recipes in your own houses, they might find their way into friends' houses too.

Schweizer Spitzen
Swiss peaks

MAKES ABOUT 30

A celebratory chocolate that looks show-stoppingly good, yet is a cinch to make. In Germany, Kirschwasser, a double-distilled morello cherry brandy, is often used in conjunction with chocolate, most famously in a Schwarzwälder Kirschtorte, and these little Swiss peaks are no exception – sometimes I also sit a sour cherry at the bottom of the foil case before piping the chocolate in.

100ml (7 tbsp) double (heavy) cream
200g (7oz) dark chocolate (50% cocoa solids), broken into pieces

30g (2 tbsp) unsalted butter or coconut oil
1 tbsp *Kirschwasser* or cherry brandy

eat the cream in a saucepan over a medium heat, stirring from time to time to avoid it scorching on the bottom. Take it off the heat just before it comes to a boil. Add the chocolate and butter or coconut oil and stir with a wooden spoon until both are dissolved. Mix in the *Kirschwasser* and beat for a minute until smooth and glossy. Refrigerate for 45 minutes so that it stiffens up slightly.

Lay out small foil chocolate cases on a baking sheet. Give the mixture a good stir through again then spoon it into a piping bag fitted with a 1cm/⅜in star-shaped nozzle. Pipe the mixture, with a swirling motion, into the foil cases, lifting the nozzle up at the very end to create a peak.

Stored in an airtight container, these will keep well for 2 weeks. They don't need to be refrigerated but I think they're particularly good when a little cold, so I like to refrigerate them 15 minutes before serving.

Espresso-Eiskonfekt
Espresso refrigerator chocolates

MAKES ABOUT 30

These chocolates are a grown-up take on a beloved childhood confection, Eiskonfekt.

Traditionally they are made with cocoa powder but I find using chocolate easier and the end results comparable to the original. These are popular all year round in Germany, but especially when there is snow on the ground – the little tin moulds are gently pressed into the snow and left there until the chocolate sets.

200g (7oz) dark chocolate (70% cocoa solids), broken into pieces
3 tbsp coconut oil

2 tbsp strong espresso
About 1 tbsp icing (confectioners') sugar
30 coffee beans

ut the chocolate, coconut oil and espresso into a saucepan and melt over a gentle heat, stirring constantly. Once everything has melted, add a teaspoon of the icing sugar, stir through and taste for sweetness, adding a little more if it isn't sweet enough for your tastes.

Pour the mixture into greaseproof mini-bon-bon cases (or an ice-cube tray will do) and top each with a coffee bean. Allow to cool a little before refrigerating for 3 hours until set. If you have used an ice-cube tray you will need to turn it upside down and tap it very gently on the work surface to release the chocolates. Be careful when transferring them to a dish, as they melt very easily when touched with warm hands.

These keep well stored in a covered container in the fridge for up to 3 weeks.

Rumkugeln
Rum balls

MAKES 24

*My brother Oliver's favourite. I tried for years to create rum truffles
with a fudgy texture and never succeeded until writing this book,
where I found the answer in front of me on the kitchen table – porridge
oats. Ground finely to a 'flour', oats soak up and retain the moisture
of the oil and rum in these balls, giving them the perfect bite.*

*The alcohol will be very strong initially but becomes mellower after
a few hours, so it's a good idea to leave a little time between making
and serving them. I don't like these to be too sweet myself,
but add more icing sugar to suit your own tastes should
you prefer a sweeter confection.*

65g (⅔ cup) porridge
   oats
6 tbsp coconut oil or
   unsalted butter
45g (1½oz)
   unsweetened cocoa
   powder

85g (½ cup plus 3 tbsp)
   icing (confectioners')
   sugar
3 tbsp dark rum
70g (2½oz) chocolate
   sprinkles

Put the oats into a food processor and blitz to a fine, flour-like powder.

Melt the coconut oil in a small saucepan over a medium heat. Once melted, take off the heat and sift in the cocoa powder and icing sugar, stirring until evenly mixed. Add the ground oats and rum and beat everything with a wooden spoon until a soft, pliable 'truffle' forms.

Put the chocolate sprinkles into a shallow dish. Pinch off teaspoon-sized chunks of the truffle mixture and roll into small balls between the palms of your hands. Roll each ball in the sprinkles so that they are coated all over.

Stored in an airtight tin, these will keep well for at least 3 weeks.

Mandelsplitter
Almond chocolates

MAKES ABOUT 12

*A favourite traditional 'chocolate box' chocolate that is almost
as easy to make at home as it is to select out of the box.*

100g (3½oz) dark
  chocolate (70%
  cocoa solids),
  broken into pieces
¼ tsp coconut oil

100g (3½oz) blanched
  almonds, roughly
  chopped
Finely grated zest of
  ½ orange

ine a baking sheet with non-stick
baking parchment.

Put the almonds into a frying pan
(skillet) and toast over a medium
heat for a few minutes until golden in colour
and a nutty aroma arises from the pan, stirring
occasionally with a wooden spoon to avoid
burning. Remove from the pan and set aside
to cool.

Put the chocolate and coconut oil into a
heatproof bowl. Place the bowl over a small
saucepan with a 1cm/⅜in depth of water in the
bottom. Turn the heat on low and wait for the
chocolate to melt. Once the chocolate starts
melting, stir it so that the coconut oil is evenly
dispersed and it's viscous and glossy.

Take off the heat, add the almonds and orange
zest and stir until everything is coated in
chocolate.

Take heaped teaspoons of the mixture and
place on the prepared sheet, in baton shapes
4cm/1½in long.

Allow the chocolates to cool completely on
the sheet – this can take up to 3 hours – before
storing in an airtight container, where they will
keep well for around 2 weeks.

Pfefferminztaler
Peppermint fondants

These are as German as they are British, and they're also my husband's favourite, which makes them a confection I'm particularly fond of. Fondant actually plays as prominent a role during Easter celebrations in Germany as it does at Christmas time. Peppermint is the main Christmas flavouring and small bite-sized pieces are often dipped in chocolate, while fruit-flavoured fondant is made into wreath shapes. At Easter time the fondant is either flavoured with fruit or alcohol, and formed into chicks, (fried) eggs and birds' nests.

300g (2 cups plus 2 tbsp) icing (confectioners') sugar, sifted

1 egg white
½ tsp peppermint extract

ine a baking sheet with non-stick baking parchment.

Mix all the ingredients together in a bowl until a thick fondant is formed.

Take teaspoon-sized pieces of fondant and roll them into balls between the palms of your hands. Place on the prepared baking sheet and press down gently on the fondant balls with the prongs of a fork until flattened into button shapes, around 7mm/⅓in thick.

Leave to air dry for 24 hours before boxing up, turning the fondants over after 12 hours to ensure they dry out equally on both sides.

Stored in an airtight container, these will keep well for up to a month.

NOTE

Substitute the peppermint extract for the same quantity of lemon or orange extract to create a fruit-flavoured fondant.

Marzipankonfekt

MARZIPAN SWEETS

While the country of marzipan's origins may be disputed, and Germany isn't one of them, there is no doubt that marzipan is one of Germany's most beloved confections.

The Northern German city of Lübeck, in particular, is renowned for its marzipan production, and with good cause, for *Lübecker Marzipan* is some of the finest quality marzipan in the world. It is made with a high percentage of almonds to sugar and manufacturers within the city have strict quantity guidelines to adhere to.

In German baking, an ingredient called *Marzipanrohmasse* is used more frequently than marzipan itself. *Marzipanrohmasse* is an almond paste and has far fewer added ingredients than commercial marzipan. It's softer and more crumbly in texture than marzipan, which is often enhanced with egg white or glucose syrup to give it a pliable texture and pleasant mouthfeel. It's not easy to get hold of in the UK but the homemade marzipan recipe I give in this chapter is actually more similar to *Marzipanrohmasse* than it is to commercial marzipan, and is well suited to baking as well as to be enjoyed as a sweet treat.

Marzipan
Marzipan

MAKES ABOUT 280g (10oz)

I have based this marzipan recipe on the Lübecker idea of a strong almond to sugar ratio, which results in a not-too-sweet, and a softly textured, marzipan.

210g (2 cups minus 3 tbsp) ground almonds (almond flour)

90g (⅔ cup) icing (confectioners') sugar

1 tsp orange flower water

2 tsp almond extract

Put the ground almonds into a food processor and blitz them for 3–5 minutes until they clump together slightly and resemble something like fresh breadcrumbs. Add the sugar and blitz for about 3 minutes, scraping down the sides every so often.

Add the orange flower water and almond extract and blitz for a further 3–5 minutes until it comes together into a ball. It's important not to over-blitz, as this will bring out too much of the almond oil – check on the dough every minute by stopping the machine and pinching some mixture together to see how easily it will come together into a marzipan mass.

This will keep well for up to 3 weeks if wrapped in a freezer bag and stored in an airtight tin.

Marzipan-Datteln mit Mandeln
Marzipan and almond stuffed dates

MAKES 15–20 (DEPENDING ON THE SIZE OF YOUR DATES)

More of an assembly job than a recipe, and unlike flat-pack furniture, this one does not come with rigid instructions. You can chop and change ingredients so what you end up 'building' will look and be unique to your tastes.

15–20 Medjool dates (or pitted prunes, dried apricots or figs)

200g (7oz) golden marzipan (alternatively, use the marzipan recipe opposite)

Finely grated zest of ½ orange

15 blanched almonds (or walnut pieces/halves)

Slit the dates lengthwise down one side and take the stones (pits) out.

In a small bowl, mix the marzipan with the orange zest – I find the best way to do this is to squeeze it in my fists. Divide the marzipan into 15–20 pieces (depending on how many dates you have), roll them into little sausage shapes and fit one into the hollow of each date. Press a nut into the centre.

Stored in an airtight container, these will keep for 2 weeks.

Walnussmarzipan
Chocolate-coated walnut marzipan

These little sweets came about one autumn when we found the ground on our usual path to school scattered with walnuts. After dropping the boys off I rushed home, scooping up as many nuts along the way as I could carry.

Back in the kitchen all sorts of walnut creations took place; this one I wrote down in my notebook for Christmas. The flavours come from a German-Polish border biscuit that Helga, our late German neighbour in Wales, used to put on her Bunter Teller. I asked her one year for the recipe, but she was reluctant to pass it on. The biscuit base was spread with apricot jam, a layer of marzipan next, followed by half a walnut crown all wrapped up in a glaze of vodka icing.

In one bite-sized biscuit, they swept me directly to cold snowy cobbled streets with people's breath hanging in clouds under the glow of street lamps. There was just something about them that seemed so old-fashioned that was hard to put my finger on — the vodka somehow brought a mysterious feeling of cold into your mouth.

200g (7oz) walnuts (or walnut pieces)
75g (½ cup plus ½ tbsp) icing (confectioners') sugar, sifted
1–2 tbsp vodka

180g (6oz) dark chocolate
¼ tsp coconut oil
Flaky sea salt, to sprinkle on top

Place the walnuts in a food processor and blitz for about 2 minutes until finely ground, then scrape down the sides of the processor and blitz again for a couple of minutes until the oils are released from the nuts and the mixture begins to clump together.

Add the icing sugar along with 1 tablespoon of vodka and blitz again until a smooth paste forms. You may need to add a bit more vodka depending on how fresh the nuts are.

Form the marzipan into a rectangle 1cm/⅜in deep and refrigerate for 30 minutes.

Put the chocolate and coconut oil into a heatproof bowl and place the bowl over a small saucepan with a 1cm/⅜in depth of water in the bottom. Turn the heat on low and wait for the chocolate to melt. Once it starts melting, stir so that the coconut oil is evenly dispersed. Take off the heat once the chocolate is glossy and fluid.

Line a baking sheet with non-stick baking parchment.

Cut the marzipan into 1cm/⅜in squares and, using a fork held horizontally with the tines pointing upwards to balance the marzipan on, dip each square carefully into the chocolate, so that it is completely covered. Lift gently onto the baking paper and continue until all squares are covered. Sprinkle each square with a little flaky sea salt and allow to set before boxing up.

Stored in an airtight container, these keep well for up to a week.

Marzipankartoffeln
Marzipan 'potatoes'

MAKES 25

Marzipan disguised as potatoes are a traditional Christmas confection in Germany – I really don't know why or how these originally came about, as potatoes aren't particularly festive, but we love them in our house. There isn't much to making them really, but I've included them in this book because they're such an integral part of German Advent rituals.

½ tsp unsweetened cocoa powder

200g (7oz) golden marzipan (see page 230 for homemade)

Put the cocoa powder into a medium bowl. Pinch off pieces of marzipan the size of hazelnuts (in shells) and roll them into balls between the palms of your hands, then place in the bowl of cocoa. Once all of the marzipan is rolled, make circular motions with the bowl so that the marzipan starts to roll around and is covered in cocoa. The idea, of course, is that the cocoa looks like the mud on the outside of the potatoes, so it doesn't need to be perfectly covered, and don't worry either if your balls get slightly knocked out of shape; this all adds to the potato's charm.

Stored in an airtight container, these will keep well for 2 weeks.

Weihnachtsgetränke

FESTIVE DRINKS

No form of Christmas festivities should take place without a drink in hand. Aside from the obvious outdoor activities such as sledging and the likes, for which a drink is best had afterwards, everything from carol singing to tree decorating and board gaming with the family is made that bit better with a glass or mug alongside.

It doesn't always need to be alcoholic, although I find the alcohol helps sometimes at extended family gatherings — if you too can relate to this, then I highly recommend the *Weihnachtsschnaps*. *Schnapps* aside, herbal teas are actually one of the nation's favourite drinks, and these days many people choose black tea or a fruitier version over a cup of coffee. The selection of herbal and fruit-flavoured teas in German supermarkets is mind-boggling and stalls dedicated to an eclectic mix of tea are present at many Christmas markets. My favourite festive tea is simply made out of the peel of the many satsumas we eat over Advent. I slice the peel finely and lay it out on sheets to air dry for a couple of days; once dried, it keeps well for over a year if stored in an airtight tin. Add some dried rosehips to the satsuma peel too and you'll have a herbal tea rich in vitamin C.

So, despite primarily being a baking book, it occurred to me early on while writing that every single biscuit and cake recipe within these pages goes hand in hand with a drink of some sort or other. Here are some of our favourite ski-slope and *Weihnachtsmarkt*-inspired beverages.

Glühwein
Mulled wine

MAKES ABOUT 750ML (3 CUPS)

It's not to everyone's taste – I'm sure wine buffs out there think it's an absolute disgrace – but to many of us Glühwein is a firm Christmas favourite. I have to admit there are lots of drinks I prefer, but despite this, Glühwein still holds a special place in my heart around the festive season.

I keep the spicing simple, but you can add a vanilla pod, nutmeg, allspice berries and star anise to the saucepan as well, should you wish for an alternative, less traditional flavour.

1 bottle of fruity red wine (it really shouldn't be anything special)	10 cloves
2 cinnamon sticks (each about 7cm/2¾in)	Pared zest of 1 orange (use a swivel peeler) 75g (6 tbsp) granulated sugar

ut all the ingredients into a large saucepan over a high heat. Stir with a wooden spoon until the sugar is dissolved. Cook until piping hot, but turn off the heat as it comes to a simmer. Place a lid on the pan and let the wine rest on the stovetop for 10 minutes, giving the spices time to mingle and for the wine to be the right serving temperature.

I don't bother straining it, as I feel a clove bobbing up and down in your glass adds to the fun of it and a strip of orange zest looks rather pretty, but by all means strain it if you prefer.

Kinderpunsch
Non-alcoholic punch

MAKES ABOUT 1 LITRE (4½ CUPS)

Children and adults alike love this festive non-alcoholic version of Glühwein.

1 litre (4 cups) red grape juice	2 cinnamon sticks (each about 7cm/2¾in)
8 cloves	1 orange, sliced 5mm/⅛in thick
1 star anise	

ut all the ingredients into a large saucepan over a high heat. Cook until piping hot, but turn the heat off as it comes to a simmer. Place a lid on the pan and let the *Kinderpunsch* rest on the stovetop for 10 minutes, giving the spices some time to mingle and for the punch to be the right serving temperature.

This is also delicious cold. If you do have some left over and want to keep if for the next day, be sure to take the spices out as otherwise it will end up being too strongly flavoured.

Weihnachtsschnaps
Christmas Schnapps

MAKES ABOUT 1 LITRE (4½ CUPS)

The perfect pick-me-up, I keep a bottle of it in the fridge door and enjoy
it like a sort of 'espresso' or mixed with milk or fresh orange juice.

FOR THE CHRISTMAS
SCHNAPPS
500ml (2 cups) vodka
125g (⅔ cup) demerara
  sugar (or more if you
  like it sweeter)
1 cinnamon stick
Pared zest of 1 orange
  (use a swivel peeler)
1 vanilla pod (bean),
  split lengthwise
20g (¾oz) coffee
  beans, cracked in a
  mortar with a pestle

WITH ORANGE
50ml (3½ tbsp)
  Christmas Schnapps
Juice of 1 orange
1 tbsp lemon juice

WITH MILK
25ml (2 tbsp minus
  1 tsp) Christmas
  Schnapps
50ml (3½ tbsp) whole
  milk

To make the Christmas *Schnapps*, put all the ingredients into a large glass jar, seal and shake the bottle over the course of a week from day to day to dissolve the sugar. Strain through a muslin (cheesecloth) or coffee filter, and bottle.

Prepare as below. This is also good poured over ice cream, added to coffee or used in cakes and desserts.

CHRISTMAS *SCHNAPPS* WITH ORANGE

Fill an old fashioned glass with ice, pour over the Christmas *Schnapps* followed by the orange then lemon juice, stir and enjoy.

CHRISTMAS *SCHNAPPS* WITH MILK

Mix the Christmas *Schnapps* with the milk and pour into a short glass filled with ice.

Feuerzangenbowle 'Fire tongs' punch

MAKES ABOUT 2 LITRES (8½ CUPS)

A Feuerzangenbowle *is as much about the ceremony and process as it is about the actual drink itself – it's a party piece and one that demands everyone's attention.*

A Zuckerhut *(sugar cone) soaked in rum is placed onto tongs above a bowl of warm spiced wine, and is then set on fire so that it caramelizes and drips into the wine below.*

Many households own a special bowl for this, which has a stand with a tea-light holder underneath and a sugar tong attachment for the top, but you can do this without any special equipment – all you need is a large saucepan, a tea-light warmer and hand-held metal grater to balance on top of the saucepan.

The Feuerzangenbowle's *season is very short, as traditionally it is only drunk at Christmas and on New Year's Eve, after which our bowl goes back up into the attic along with all the decorations.*

It's important that the rum has an alcohol content of at least 54% otherwise it won't catch fire. Also – health and safety warning – if you are topping up the rum while the sugar is alight, never do this straight from the bottle; always top up using rum from a ladle.

2 oranges
1 lemon
3 bottles of fruity red
 wine
2 cinnamon sticks (each
 about 7cm/2¾in)
15 cloves

2 star anise
1 × 250g (9oz)
 Zuckerhut or 250g
 (9oz) sugar cubes
 (brown or white)
75ml (6 tbsp) rum

 sing a swivel peeler, peel strips of zest off the oranges and lemon and place in a large saucepan. Now squeeze the oranges and lemon and pour the juice into the saucepan.

Add the wine, cinnamon sticks, cloves and star anise to the pan and warm over a high heat until piping hot but not boiling. Turn off the heat, put a lid on the saucepan and let it rest for 5 minutes to give the spices some time to permeate the wine.

Light the tea light underneath the bowl/saucepan that you intend to serve this from. Pour the warm spiced wine into the bowl or pan. Rest the sugar tongs or grater on top of the bowl and place the *Zuckerhut* (or sugar cubes) in the middle. Pour the rum slowly over the sugar so that it sinks in, then light a match and set fire to it. The flame will be blue and it might dim after a while, in which case top up with more rum from a ladle.

Once the sugar has melted, remove the tongs and stir the wine until all the sugar has dissolved. It will stay warm so long as the tea light underneath is lit. Serve in heatproof glass mugs.

Heißer Kakao mit Rum
Hot chocolate with rum

SERVES 1

My great-grandmother always started her hot cocoa off with water before adding the milk, so my mother tells me, and so, now, do I — partly because I like to keep these little kitchen quirks going, but also, mainly, because it really is better this way.

2 tsp unsweetened cocoa powder
1 tbsp just-boiled water
150ml (10 tbsp) whole milk
1 tbsp dark brown sugar

25ml (2 tbsp minus 1 tsp) dark rum or brandy

TO TOP
Whipped cream
Grated chocolate

Mix the cocoa and hot water together thoroughly in a mug. Add the milk to the mug and stir. Put the sugar into a small saucepan and then pour over the cocoa mixture. Heat over a medium-high heat, stirring, until the sugar has dissolved. Take off the heat once the hot chocolate is piping hot but before it comes to a simmer.

Pour the rum into the mug and pour the hot chocolate over it, stir once, then top with whipped cream and grated chocolate.

Eierlikör
Vanilla brandy cream

MAKES JUST SHY OF 600ml (2½ CUPS)

An alcoholic egg-yolk cream might not sound too enticing, which is why I haven't called it that — eggs in a drink can be a little off-putting, but you'd never know they were there in this silky vanilla-scented liqueur, which is rather like the continental cousin of an Irish cream — and who doesn't admit to loving a Baileys at Christmas time?

Eierlikör is a typical Advent drink, also popular over the Easter period. It's served in little shot glasses made out of chocolate as a sweet treat after a meal or poured over ice cream and into coffee or hot milk with a grating of nutmeg (a quick version of an eggnog). It also works well in place of Advocaat in a snowball cocktail (I'll hold my hands up and admit to loving these too).

Traditionally this is made with the seeds of a vanilla pod — split the vanilla pod lengthwise and scrape out the seeds — but often I just use vanilla extract instead, mainly because it's much cheaper and these days it's easy to get hold of a good-quality bottle.

4 egg yolks
140g (1 cup) icing
   (confectioners') sugar
Pinch of fine sea salt
150ml (10 tbsp) brandy

1½ tsp vanilla extract
200ml (¾ cup plus
   1½ tbsp) single
   (light) cream

Put the egg yolks, icing sugar and salt into the bowl of a free-standing electric mixer fitted with a whisk attachment (or use a mixing bowl and hand-held electric whisk), and whisk for around 3 minutes until light and fluffy.

Add the brandy, vanilla extract and cream and whisk for a further 3 minutes until silky and thick. Funnel the cream into a sterilized bottle and store in the fridge, where it will keep for 2 weeks.

Karneval und Silvester

CARNIVAL AND NEW YEAR'S EVE

Karneval season in Germany spans over a few months and starts before Christmas on the 11th day of the 11th month at 11 minutes past the 11th hour, but it isn't until January and February when the celebrations really get underway to start the year off swinging.

A countrywide winter celebration before spring and Easter arrive, *Karneval* is seen as a time to keep some brightness and optimism in the depths of the darker months and to let your hair down, feast and be merry.

Silvester (New Year's Eve) and *Karneval* (or *Fasching* depending on which part of Germany you are from) both have roots in Pagan times – it's thought that they were celebrated with a lot of noise to end the winter and welcome the coming year and spring season, but these days *Karneval* has become synonymous with Catholicism – as one last blow-out before the

fast of Lent. But just as Christmas is celebrated by many, whether we hold religious beliefs or not, so is *Karneval*.

Everyone dresses up in costumes and fancy dress and the general mood is incredibly jolly. Many people wear masks (another hangover from Pagan times when scary costumes were worn to ward off evil spirits for the coming agricultural year) and part of the fun of the festivities is guessing who's underneath which disguise. There are parades, gatherings on the streets and parties to end all parties. I'd take a chance at guessing people drink more during *Karneval* than at *Oktoberfest*. Dancing and singing are commonplace, in fact they are highly encouraged, as are poetry recitals and satirical speeches.

Continued overleaf

The city of *Köln* (Cologne) boasts some of the most lively and colourful *Karneval* celebrations in Germany and I'm lucky to have experienced many great parties at this time of year while staying there with friends. It's a magical time to witness all the adults go crazy, giving many children a glimpse of the other side to *Mama und Papa*, usually reserved for after-hours.

While *Karneval* officially starts in November, it's mainly just organization (these colossal parties don't happen without a bit of planning) rather than celebrating that happens before the New year. *Silvester* (New Year's Eve), for me, is when everybody really starts getting into the silliness and *Karneval* mood.

The traditional supper at *Silvester* is carp, but today many Germans take inspiration from their Swiss neighbours and make *Raclette* or *Fondue* instead, which I personally find much more appetizing and fun, not least because white wine, beer and *Schnapps* are recommended to accompany the last cheese-rich meal of the year. Lentil soup is also a popular New Year's Eve or Day dish, each spoonful of coin-shaped lentils believed to be a sign of riches for the year ahead — double up with sausages cut into 'coins' and you'll have twice the prosperity.

For dessert *Berliner* (jam-filled doughnuts — see opposite) are piled high on plates to be eaten later on in the evening. If hosting a party to see in the new year, it is custom to fill one of the doughnuts with mustard instead of jam as a prank — children delight in this and watch carefully as each person takes a bite into the pillowy, sugar-coated fried dough.

To drink a *Feuerzangenbowle* (see page 242) is both potent and entertaining. It consists of warm, spiced red wine over which a rum-soaked sugar 'hat' is set on fire, so that the sugar caramelizes and drips into the wine below — it's one of the best ways to get any party started and is part of a classic German New Year's Eve celebration.

At midnight fireworks light up the sky across each city, and if you're out and about celebrating you'll be in for quite a show, as many people carry fireworks with them in their pockets ready to set light to on the pavements just as the clock strikes twelve.

One of my favourite New Year's Eve traditions is *Bleigießen*, a form of fortune telling done by melting little lead (now tin or wax for safety) figures in spoons over a candle. Once the lead has melted it is poured into a bowl of cold water; whatever shape your spoonful of lead solidifies into predicts your fortune for the coming year: a ball shape, for example, means luck will come your way; a flower means new friendships will blossom; a feather means change is afoot; a cake means you'll have reason to celebrate...

Berliner
Jam-filled doughnuts

MAKES 12

*It's not often that we deep-fry food at home, but we like to make
Berliner on New Year's Eve. While it's custom to fill one with mustard
instead of the regular jam, to surprise an unsuspecting guest with, I'm
yet to bring myself round to doing it – it seems such a waste when you
go to all the effort of making them in the first place. Never say never,
though – I'm sure as soon as our boys catch wind of this tradition
they won't let me get away with holding back on the potential fun.*

*These doughnuts are coated twice with sugar, first with fine caster
and then with icing sugar, which makes them particularly moreish.*

250g (1¾ cups plus 2 tbsp) plain (all-purpose) flour, plus extra for dusting
250g (1¾ cups) strong white bread flour
1 tbsp caster (superfine) sugar
½ tsp fine sea salt
90g (6 tbsp) unsalted butter, at room temp
4 egg yolks
40g (1½oz) fresh yeast, or 20g (¾oz) dried

180ml (¾ cup) tepid whole milk
1 litre (4½ cups) sunflower oil, for deep-frying, plus extra for greasing

TO COAT AND FILL
Caster (superfine) sugar and icing (confectioners') sugar
½ jar of jam (jelly) – I like to use plum, but any red jam is good

Using a pastry brush, oil a large baking sheet with sunflower oil.

Put both flours, the sugar and salt into a large bowl and mix together with a wooden spoon. Add the butter and egg yolks to the bowl. Crumble the yeast (or sprinkle if using dried) into the tepid milk and stir to dissolve. Pour the yeasted milk into the flour mixture and, using your hands, bring everything together into a rough dough. Tip the dough out onto a lightly floured surface and knead for about 10 minutes until it becomes more elastic. Form it into a ball and nestle it into the bottom of the bowl. Cover the bowl with a tea towel and set aside in a warm spot to rise for 1–3 hours until almost doubled in size. (Alternatively, put the flour, sugar and salt into the bowl of a free-standing electric mixer fitted with a dough hook. Add the butter and egg yolks. Pour in the yeasted milk and knead for 5 minutes until elastic. Cover and set aside, as above.)

Knock the dough back with your fist and divide it into four equal pieces. Take one piece and split it into three pieces. Mould each piece into a ball and place well apart, to allow room for spreading, on the prepared baking sheet. Repeat this process with the remaining dough. Lay a tea towel gently over the sheet and set aside in a warm spot for 30 minutes–1 hour, to rise for a second time. You want the balls to have at least doubled in size.

Continued overleaf

Line a shallow dish with kitchen paper and spread a couple of tablespoons of caster sugar in a second shallow dish.

Pour enough oil into a large, heavy-based saucepan for deep-frying, making sure the pan is no more than two-thirds full, and heat to 170°C/338°F, or when a cube of bread dropped into it sizzles on impact and starts to turn golden after a few seconds.

Working in batches (I usually fry three at a time), gently lower the doughnuts into the hot oil and fry for 2–3 minutes on each side until golden brown all over.

Remove the *Berliner* from the oil, using a slotted spoon, and place on the kitchen paper to soak up any excess oil, then transfer to the dish with the sugar and roll around until well coated.

Place on a wire rack to cool while you repeat this process with the rest of the doughnuts.

Once the doughnuts are cool enough to handle, you can fill them with the jam. I usually put the jam into a freezer bag, then cut a little snip off the corner, but you can of course just use a piping bag.

Insert a chopstick into the side of each doughnut by a couple of centimetres/an inch or so and wiggle it slightly to create a hole. Place the nozzle end of the bag into the hole left by the chopstick and squirt about a tablespoon of jam inside. Sprinkle them all with icing sugar and they are ready to serve.

These are best eaten the day they are made, but if wrapped well they will still be fine the next day too.

Käsestangen mit Kümmel
Caraway cheese straws

MAKES ABOUT 60

It isn't a party if there aren't cheese crackers on the table, or that's what I think anyway. While being full of butter and cheese, these are deceptively light and it's best to keep them small.

50g (6 tbsp) rye flour
50g (6 tbsp) plain
 (all-purpose) flour,
 plus extra for dusting
Pinch of fine sea salt
½ tsp sweet paprika
80g (⅓ cup plus
 1 tsp) unsalted butter,
 at room temp

1 egg yolk
½ tsp caraway seeds
80g (3oz) mature
 Cheddar or Emmental,
 grated

Heat the oven to 180°C/160°C fan/350°F and line a large baking sheet with non-stick baking parchment.

Put both flours, the salt and sweet paprika into a bowl and mix together. Add the butter and work it in with your fingertips until the mixture resembles breadcrumbs. Now add the egg yolk, caraway seeds and grated cheese. Knead everything together into a dough.

Dust the work surface with flour and roll the dough out to around 3mm/⅛in thick. Cut out strips that are 7cm/2¾in long and 1cm/⅜in wide. I don't worry about the edges looking scraggly; I actually quite like the variety of the misshapen ones. Lay carefully on the prepared baking sheet, leaving around 1cm/⅜in between each.

Bake for 10–12 minutes until golden brown. Allow to cool on the sheet for a couple of minutes before transferring to a wire rack to cool completely.

Stored in an airtight tin, these will keep well for 2 weeks. I guarantee you won't have them dangling around for that long, though.

Also pictured: Weihnachtsschmalzgebäck *(p.81)*

Glücksbringer
Lucky charms

MAKES ABOUT 35

These little biscuits are full of New Year's luck — shaped like coins for prosperity, full of gold from the egg yolk and decorated with a 'lucky' mushroom — you're bound to have a good year ahead if you eat one.

150g (1 cup plus
   2 tbsp) plain
   (all-purpose) flour
Pinch of fine sea salt
80g (⅓ cup plus
   1 tsp) unsalted butter,
   at room temp
50g (6 tbsp) icing
   (confectioners') sugar,
   plus extra for dusting
   and icing

2 egg yolks
½ tsp vanilla extract
Milk, for brushing

TO DECORATE
Flaked (slivered)
   almonds
Glacé cherries, halved

Heat the oven to 190°C/170°C fan/375°F and line two large baking sheets with non-stick baking parchment.

Put the flour, salt and butter into a mixing bowl and, using your fingertips, work the butter into the flour until the mixture resembles breadcrumbs. Add the icing sugar and mix it through. Now add the egg yolks and vanilla extract and bring everything together into a dough with your hands. Knead for a few minutes.

Dust the work surface with icing sugar and roll the dough out to a 3mm/⅛in thickness. Using a fluted cookie cutter (see pages 258–9), cut out circles and place on the prepared baking sheets, leaving 1cm/⅜in between each. Re-roll all the dough offcuts into more biscuits. Brush the top of each with milk and place one flaked almond on the biscuit with one point in the centre.

Bake for 8–10 minutes until golden brown. Let the biscuits cool on the sheet for a minute before transferring to a wire rack to cool completely.

Lay a glacé cherry half on the centre end of each almond to create a mushroom top.

Mix 1 tablespoon of icing sugar with a couple of drops of water to create a thick paste. Use the prong of a fork or a cocktail stick (toothpick) to dip into the icing. Now dot the iced prong onto the glacé cherry to create little white spots on the red 'mushroom'.

Cookie cutters

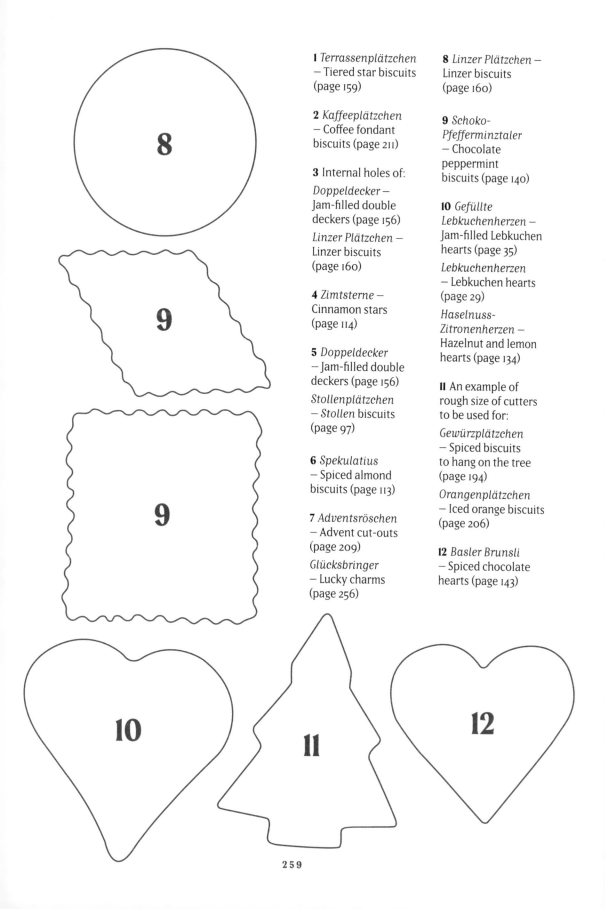

1 *Terrassenplätzchen* – Tiered star biscuits (page 159)

2 *Kaffeeplätzchen* – Coffee fondant biscuits (page 211)

3 Internal holes of:
Doppeldecker – Jam-filled double deckers (page 156)
Linzer Plätzchen – Linzer biscuits (page 160)

4 *Zimtsterne* – Cinnamon stars (page 114)

5 *Doppeldecker* – Jam-filled double deckers (page 156)
Stollenplätzchen – Stollen biscuits (page 97)

6 *Spekulatius* – Spiced almond biscuits (page 113)

7 *Adventsröschen* – Advent cut-outs (page 209)
Glücksbringer – Lucky charms (page 256)

8 *Linzer Plätzchen* – Linzer biscuits (page 160)

9 *Schoko-Pfefferminztaler* – Chocolate peppermint biscuits (page 140)

10 *Gefüllte Lebkuchenherzen* – Jam-filled Lebkuchen hearts (page 35)
Lebkuchenherzen – Lebkuchen hearts (page 29)
Haselnuss-Zitronenherzen – Hazelnut and lemon hearts (page 134)

11 An example of rough size of cutters to be used for:
Gewürzplätzchen – Spiced biscuits to hang on the tree (page 194)
Orangenplätzchen – Iced orange biscuits (page 206)

12 *Basler Brunsli* – Spiced chocolate hearts (page 143)

Vegan recipe index

(OR SIMPLE SWITCHES TO MAKE VEGAN)

Gluten-free recipe index

(OR SIMPLE SWITCHES TO MAKE GLUTEN-FREE)

Index

Thank you and Merry Christmas

Steven, I can't thank you enough for 23 years of love, and for supporting any creative endeavours I undertake. The linocuts in this book are dedicated to you.

Lucas, Bia and Aidan, my Dunklings and expert biscuit testers, your enthusiasm for Advent is written all over these pages.

Pete, *Advent* was born out of your idea for a German Christmas baking book, thank you for planting the seed.

Emily Sweet, my agent, thank you for everything you've put into *Advent* and everything in between. I couldn't do it without you.

Sarah Lavelle — thank you for believing in *Advent* and for giving me the opportunity to illustrate as well as write recipes.

Harriet and Emily, I've loved every second of working so closely with you both on the words and design — what's more you've made it feel so relaxed, not like work at all, just fun.

To the rest of the team at Quadrille: Emma Marijewycz, Laura Willis, Laura Eldridge and everyone in the production department who've worked so hard to source cloth and finishes to make this book as beautiful as possible, Thank you.

Sally Somers — thank you for sweeping through the recipes and for the conversions.

Sarit and Itamar — thank you for your encouragement and support over the years, it has fuelled my creativity and helped me realize this dream of illustrating a book.

Jenny Ship, your kindness and generosity shines so brightly. This cover is totally inspired by you and your wooden wreath.

Kelly, moon mama and epic friend — thank you for your support, creative energy, love and coffee during the making of this book.

Vera — thank you for constantly inspiring me; Oliver, Leon and Iris, thank you for your testing.

Clare — thank you for everything, always.

Richard, Ethan and Eli — thank you for being part of our family, for sharing our kitchen table during lockdown and for helping us get through the mounds of biscuits.

Mum and Dad, I'm so lucky to have you as parents. Dad, thank you for making me feel like everything is possible. Mama, I'm eternally grateful for you, words can't do how I feel justice. You know though.

About the author

Anja Dunk was born in Wales to a German mother and a Welsh father. Her love of food began with baking and preserving alongside her mother and grandmother in their Welsh-Bavarian family kitchens, and has grown and developed through her work in cafés and restaurants over the years. She is now a freelance cook, food writer and artist.

Anja has co-written a book on preserves, *Do Preserve: Make your own jams, chutneys, pickles and cordials* (Do Book Co., 2016) and likes to share her preserving knowledge through pop-up events and workshops. She is also the author of *Strudel, Noodles and Dumplings: The new taste of German cooking* (Fourth Estate, 2018).

PUBLISHING DIRECTOR   Sarah Lavelle

JUNIOR COMMISSIONING EDITOR   Harriet Webster

SENIOR DESIGNER   Emily Lapworth

PHOTOGRAPHER & ILLUSTRATOR   Anja Dunk

FOOD & PROP STYLIST   Anja Dunk

HEAD OF PRODUCTION   Stephen Lang

PRODUCTION CONTROLLER   Sabeena Atchia

Published in 2021 by Quadrille,
an imprint of Hardie Grant Publishing

Quadrille
52–54 Southwark Street
London SE1 1UN
quadrille.com

Cataloguing in Publication Data: a catalogue record
for this book is available from the British Library.

ISBN 978 1 78713 726 4

Reprinted in 2022, 2023
10 9 8 7 6 5 4 3

Printed in China